Times Gone By

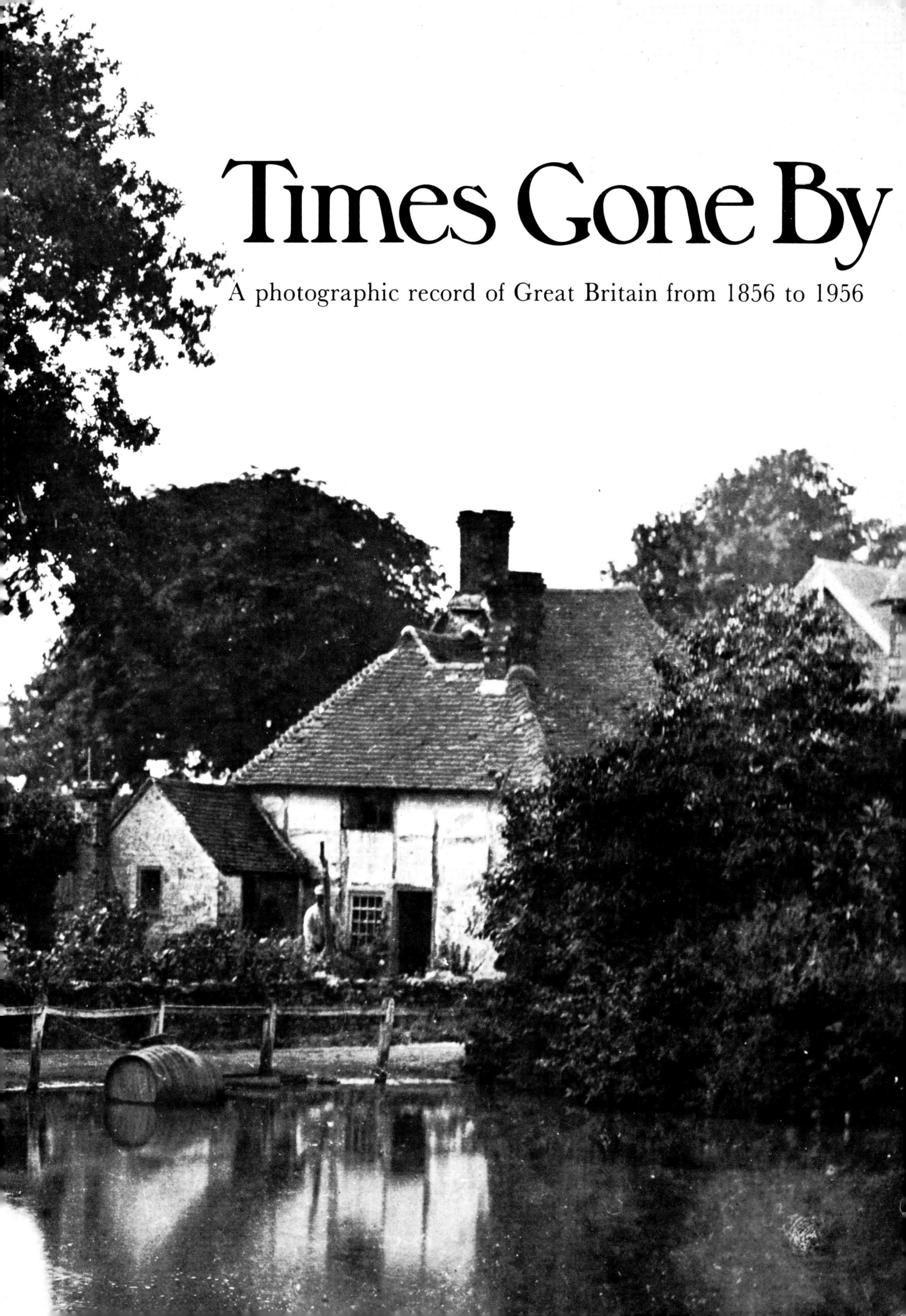

Times Gone By

A photographic record of Great Britain from 1856 to 1956

The photographs in this book have been selected to portray life in Britain during one of the most remarkable periods of her history. Many of the photographs are famous, taken from such collections as William Grundy's English Views, the Downey collection of court photographs and the London Stereoscopic collection; others are from the archives of Picture Post magazine, now sadly defunct, or the Topical Press. And it is really to the photographers themselves that most credit is due. Through their eyes we see a nation in many guises, of which some will still be familiar to us, while others will be surprising and remind us just how much times have changed.

We should like to acknowledge the help given to us by Andrew Baring in the planning of this book, and the assistance of the Librarian and staff of the Picture Company in its preparation.

The Hulton Picture Company only supplies photographs for commercial use.

Published by Marshall Cavendish Books (a division of Marshall Cavendish Partworks Limited)
119 Wardour Street
London W1V 3TD

© Marshall Cavendish Limited 1977, 1985, 1990, 1992, 1993

First Printing 1977

Editor: John Gainsford
Design: Gwyn Lewis
Picture Research: Julia Hanson

All photographs in this book are reproduced by kind permission of the Hulton Picture Company

Printed in Malaysia

ISBN 0 85685 316 X

Contents

Introduction   6

Royalty and Empire   12

Transport   40

Industry   60

Agriculture   76

Leisure   92

Home and Family   120

Politics   144

Wartime   164

Body and Soul   186

Entertainment   204

Introduction

Britain in 1856 was the richest country in the world. She had no rivals either in commerce or in industry and all the nations of the West were eager to buy her manufactured goods, to use her shipping and exploit her banking facilities. Her colonies in India, Australia, Canada and South Africa supplied her with raw materials and valuable minerals; a string of trading centres throughout the world guaranteed her commercial dominance; her powerful navy ruled the waves.

This was not the Britain of the landed aristocracy — the Britain that had built the empire. A great middle class of entrepreneurs and professional people had won control of parliament in a series of political reforms, and was moulding society in its own image. In the 1850s the principle of limited liability was firmly established, allowing the public to buy shares in companies without incurring responsibility for their debts should the venture fail. Investment soared, and businesses expanded at an unprecedented rate. Many of the newly rich built villas in the classical or the gothic style, filling their rooms with furniture and ornaments and hiring servants.

The wealthiest lived outside the smog-ridden towns, in which conditions were far from comfortable. Rapid industrialization and a rising population had resulted in large-scale migration from the rural areas to the endless rows of back-to-back terraces which housed the urban working class. Their cramped homes were flimsily built and impossible to ventilate, with extremely primitive sanitary arrangements. Outbreaks of cholera were frequent until the 1870s, when improvements ordered by the local authorities began to take effect; other diseases, such as smallpox and diphtheria, continued to thrive on undernourished, overcrowded bodies until the turn of the century.

By 1856, women and children could no longer be employed in the mines, and their working week in the textile factories had been reduced to 60 hours. Conditions for men, however, remained largely uncontrolled, and unskilled workers had little bargaining power until they formed their own trade unions. Only the skilled workers, earning over 30 shillings a week, could afford to vary a diet of bread, butter, bacon and tea with the fresh milk, meat and vegetables now brought in to the towns by train.

The railways had originally been built to transport freight, but there was great demand for the passenger trains which, by law, provided third class travel at a penny a mile. The middle classes could now take annual seaside holidays, and even a working man could go on day trips. By the late 1860s residential suburbs were being built for railway commuters.

Life in the countryside was also changing. Farmers had enjoyed a time of plenty since 1850, partly because of good weather, partly as a result of improved fertilizers and new machinery. This 'golden age' came to an end in 1878 when a bad harvest was followed by a flood of cheap corn from the North American prairies. In ten years the price of corn dropped by almost a third. At the same time the development of refrigeration meant that cheap meat could be brought from Argentina, Australia and New Zealand. Britain experienced a severe agricultural depression, followed by a change to more dairy farming and market gardening. The longer term effect of this was to encourage further the migration of people to the growing towns.

Industry suffered its own severe setback with the Great World Depression, which lasted from 1873 until the end of the century. Furthermore, the nation's industrial supremacy was now being threatened by the United States and Germany. In her search for new markets Britain joined the scramble to colonize Africa during the 1880s. At home, however, the problems could not be solved as simply, and many people were thrown out of work.

Those who remained in employment were not adversely affected by the depression. In fact there was an increase in real wages, which allowed many to take greater advantage of the expanding range of entertainments. Street showmen continued to perform songs, acrobatics and Punch and Judy shows, but the music hall proved a greater attraction. Here one could eat and drink while listening to songs ranging from the comic to the sad and the obscene. The wealthy classes went to see musical versions of the classics or pantomimes. Some played tennis, and cycling became very popular after Dunlop's invention of the pneumatic tyre in the 1880s. But their most frequent way of enjoying themselves was to sing songs round the family piano.

No more than half the population went to church regularly, but there was a strict ban on public entertainments on Sundays: even art galleries and museums were forbidden to open. This meant that working people had to rely entirely on reading if they wanted to educate themselves. For less than a shilling they could buy a standard book on almost any subject, and if they wanted fiction there were monthly magazines containing serials by authors such as Dickens. From the 1850s several newspapers provided competition for the Times, but it was not until 1896 that the first cheap, popular daily, the Daily Mail, was produced. Its combination of news and entertainment proved so successful that it soon had many imitators.

Few of the working class received a formal education. The government showed little concern about this until thousands of working men won the right to vote in 1867. A series of Acts were then passed which made education free and compulsory for all five to ten year olds. At the turn of the century, newly established local education authorities were given powers to provide secondary education and by 1918 all children aged between five and fourteen were bound to attend school. Few further changes were made before 1944, when the eleven plus exam and a three-tier system of secondary education were established.

In 1901, Queen Victoria's pleasure-loving son Edward had been crowned King. He presided over an era of transition, which saw many dramatic innovations in the sphere of technology. The telegraph and telephone had been well established during Victoria's reign, but in 1901 Marconi transmitted the first wireless message from England to America. Automobiles were still an expensive luxury, but by 1913 there were 120,000 cars in Britain, adding to the already serious congestion in the towns, where the electric tram had replaced the horse-drawn version. The spectacular 'flying machines' provided sport for a few young daredevils, but were not taken seriously by most people before the First World War.

Great strides had been made in the field of medicine since the 1850s, when nearly 60 per cent of all patients admitted to hospitals failed to survive the gruelling experience. This appalling death-rate was reduced both by scientific discoveries and by the efforts of individuals such as Florence Nightingale, who did much to improve the standards of the nursing profession and the cleanliness of hospitals. Anaesthetics began to be widely used in the 1850s and surgeons carried out many more operations, but the death-rate actually rose at first because of gangrene and tetanus. The turning point came in the 1860s when Louis Pasteur, in France, discovered that these were caused by germs, and Joseph Lister, in England, showed the benefits of disinfectants and sterilization. By the end of the century all operating theatres had been transformed. Meanwhile general medicine was revolutionized by the technique of immunization against fatal diseases.

On the eve of the First World War, Britain was more prosperous than ever before. She had a healthy trading surplus provided by invisible earnings from shipping, insurance, banking and foreign investments, and she was still the world's leading producer of textiles. Nonetheless, the future looked ominous. She had lost her lead in coal and steel production to the United States and Germany, and India and Japan were beginning to develop their own textile industries. A third of the nation continued to live in poverty; the workers, organized into trade unions, were becoming more militant in their demands for a bigger share of the nation's prosperity.

Unskilled workers had made their first successful attempts to improve conditions at the end of the 1880s, when the Bryant and May match factory girls and the London gasworkers and dockers went on strike. Then, in 1900, unions, socialist societies and co-operatives got together to establish the Labour Party, which would soon replace the Liberal Party as the chief opposition to the Conservatives. In the meantime, its representation in parliament was small, and the years 1910 to 1914 witnessed a number of national, and sometimes violent, strikes. At the same time several unions combined to form giant federations that were capable of paralysing whole industries by concerted action.

The Liberal government sought to appease the working class by introducing old age pensions and insurance against unemployment and sickness. It also abolished the right of the House of Lords to reject any bill that came before it. But the Liberals faced another challenge from middle-class women, who had been campaigning for improvements in their legal and social status throughout the Victorian era. Some had rejected a life in which they would be mere appendages of their husbands and forced a way into the professions. Others had fought for equal divorce rights and in 1882 married women had secured complete legal control over all their own property. A new departure came in 1903, when Emmeline Pankhurst founded the Women's Social and Political Union. Aware that working class women were still being paid appallingly low wages, she was determined to win political power for her sex.

She and her fellow Suffragettes won massive publicity for their cause by interrupting political meetings and being arrested. In prison they adopted the hunger strike tactic and endured forcible feeding. When this failed to win the vote, the campaign was stepped up. Empty houses and pillar boxes were burnt, windows were broken, and pictures slashed in public galleries. In 1912 the government introduced the Cat and Mouse Act, by which hunger strikers could be released just long enough to recover their health before being imprisoned again. The militant campaign continued until the outbreak of war, when the Suffragettes decided to put patriotism before women's rights. More than anything else, it was probably their contribution to the war effort that in 1918 won the vote for women over 30 years of age.

The First World War, however, had been a disaster for Britain. Nearly a million citizens were killed in the terrible carnage and those who returned faced two decades of economic gloom. After a brief period of prosperity, foreign competition began to bite and unemployment became a serious problem. Many people emigrated, to Canada, Australia or Africa; while at home, with wages actually going down, working people were moved to political action. A General Strike was called in 1926 to support the miners in their claim that they should have 'not a penny off the pay, not a minute on the day'. For ten days, in the face of the united opposition of the government, employers and middle classes, there was some solidarity amongst union members across the country. Then the miners' cause was abandoned by moderate leaders of the Trade Union Congress and the strike collapsed. The miners held out for another six months before they gave in.

Worse trouble came at the end of the decade when the Wall Street Crash sparked off another world depression, with mass unemployment in all the industrial nations of the West. By December 1930 there were 2,500,000 unemployed in Britain; dole was cut and a means test introduced to deny assistance to those with savings or a relative who could support them. The situation slowly improved in the south and Midlands where new light industries catering for the home market began to emerge. Northern England, Scotland and Wales, however, still relied on the traditional heavy industries and remained seriously depressed. Their plight was symbolized in 1936 by the march of unemployed workers from Jarrow to London.

Nonetheless, some improvements were made during the inter-war years. After 1918, local councils were encouraged to clear slums and build new houses with low rents. More than a million people were rehoused on estates where they were provided for the first time with bathrooms, gardens, gas and electricity. However, many of these estates were drab, characterless places and people missed the friendliness of their old overcrowded communities.

New entertainments also arrived. Silent movies and the 'talkies', with their romantic heroines and dashing heroes, attracted huge audiences of all ages. Dance halls, known as 'the Pally', were built in working class areas to provide regular Saturday night entertainment for the country's youth. In the 1920s, girls had flaunted their new freedom by wearing short hair and skirts, and dancing the Charleston and black bottom to the accompaniment of American jazz. By the 1930s longer skirts were back in fashion again and swing became the most popular dance music.

By 1939, over two million people owned motor cars. The mass production of the American Model T Fords, or 'Tin Lizzies', in the 1920s meant that motoring was no longer only a rich man's pastime, and country people sometimes put down glass and tacks to drive away the noisy contraptions. Working class people could club together to hire a charabanc for day trips into the countryside or to the seaside, and by the 1930s local bus services were beginning to take trade away from the railways. The number of casualties on the roads rose to an alarming extent, so a driving test was introduced in 1934.

When George VI was crowned in 1937, Britain's imperial role was dwindling fast. The government had recognised Canada, Australia, New Zealand and South Africa as self-governing dominions before the First World War; in the 1920s it went one step further, acknowledging them as Britain's equals freely associated in a Commonwealth of Nations. Relations with other parts of the Empire were less friendly. The Irish won independence after a long and bitter struggle, but the detachment of the northern counties of Ulster caused great resentment. The Indians, too, disliked their foreign rulers; Mahatma Gandhi led a campaign of civil disobedience during the twenties and thirties which gained many concessions, but not enough to secure Indian support during the Second World War. When the Labour government came to power in 1945 it was obvious that India would have to be given full independence and an act to this effect was passed in 1947.

The disintegration of the Empire was a mark of Britain's decline as a world power, a decline which was hastened by the Second World War. In 1945 the British could feel proud that they had once stood alone in opposing Nazi Germany. It was obvious, however, that the final Allied victory belonged to the United States and the Soviet Union. In the struggle, Britain's economy was ruined and, like the rest of Western Europe, she needed American aid to revive her industry and trade. The post-war years saw rising prices, food rationing, power cuts and a housing shortage.

The Labour government now laid the foundations of a new Britain. The Bank of England, the coal mines, public transport, gas, electricity and the iron and steel industries were all nationalized, and the Welfare State was fully established. The Ministry of National Insurance was made responsible not only for sickness and unemployment benefit, but also family allowances, retirement and widows' pensions, industrial injuries benefit and national assistance. At the same time the National Health Service was created, with the result that all medical and dental services became free. Henceforth, nobody would have to go without medical treatment because they could not afford it.

In 1951, however, the Conservatives were returned to power with the promise that they would bring prosperity back to Britain. And, indeed, the years of austerity were coming to an end. The motor vehicle, electrical engineering, chemical and aircraft industries were all expanding and providing new jobs in a vigorous economy. More and more people could buy cheap, mass-produced goods — for example, between the wars only the middle classes had been able to afford electric irons and vacuum cleaners, but in the fifties most families began to regard them as household essentials. Television too was entering many homes: invented before the war, its sales were boosted in 1953 when the coronation of Elizabeth II was watched by millions. The following year the Independent Television Authority was formed to compete with the British Broadcasting Corporation.

By 1956 the nation had entered a new period of prosperity. But while such marked improvements had taken place at home, Britain's international role was fast diminishing. Her decline as a world power was symbolized by the Suez crisis of 1956, when Britain attacked Egyptian airfields in reply to Egypt's closure of the Suez canal. Britain's action was condemned by most of the world; America refused to support her and she was forced to withdraw. The nation that less than a century before had been the greatest economic, commercial and imperial power in the world could no longer pursue an independent foreign policy.

Royalty
and Empire

The spread of Empire greatly enhanced the prestige of the Crown. In 1877 Victoria was delighted to be pronounced Empress of India; twenty years later much of Africa, from Cairo to the Cape, had been added to her realm.

Above A still youthful Victoria with Albert, the Prince Consort, in 1854 (believed to be the first time she was photographed).

Right British tourists on the grand tour pose in front of the Egyptian pyramids.

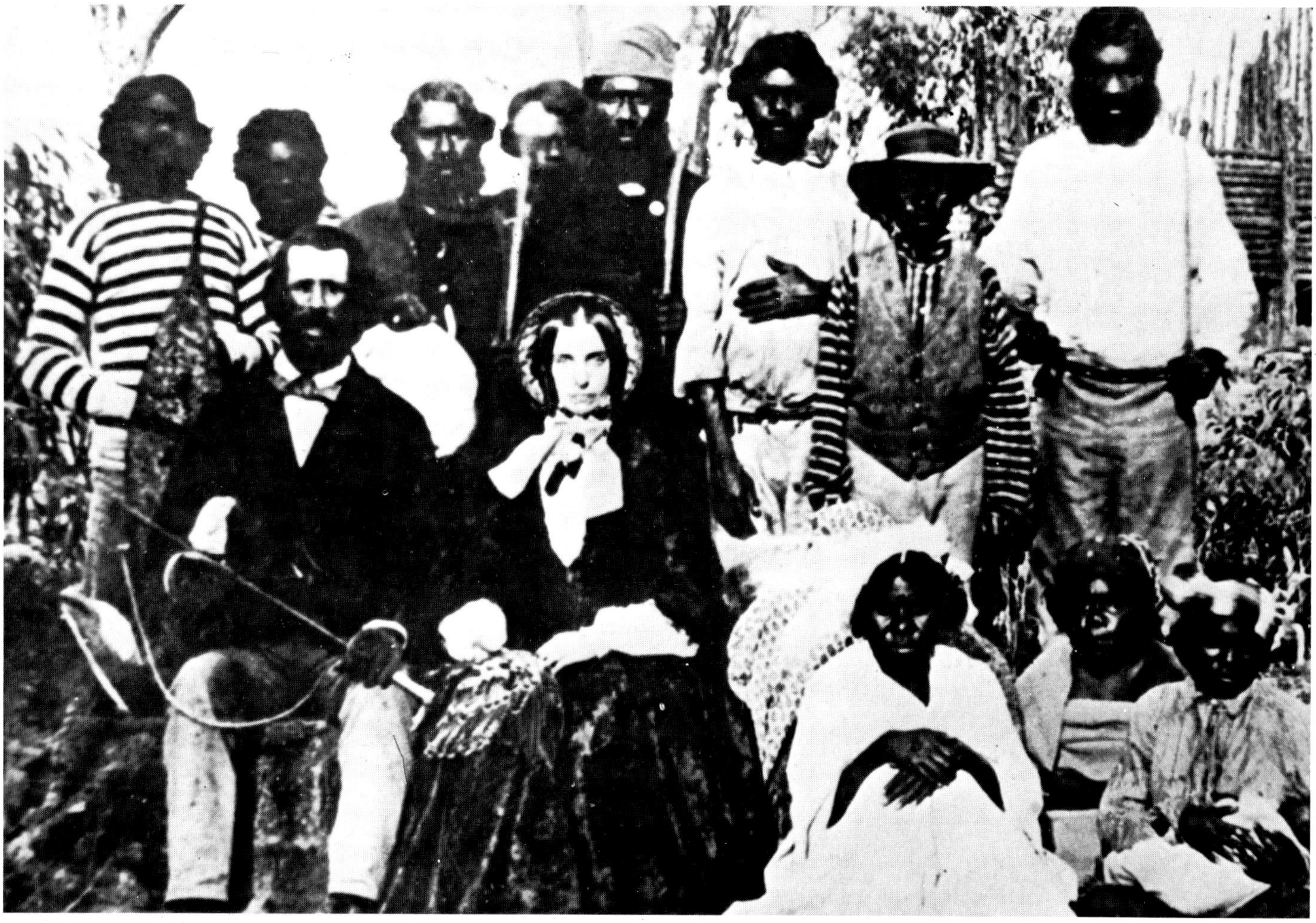

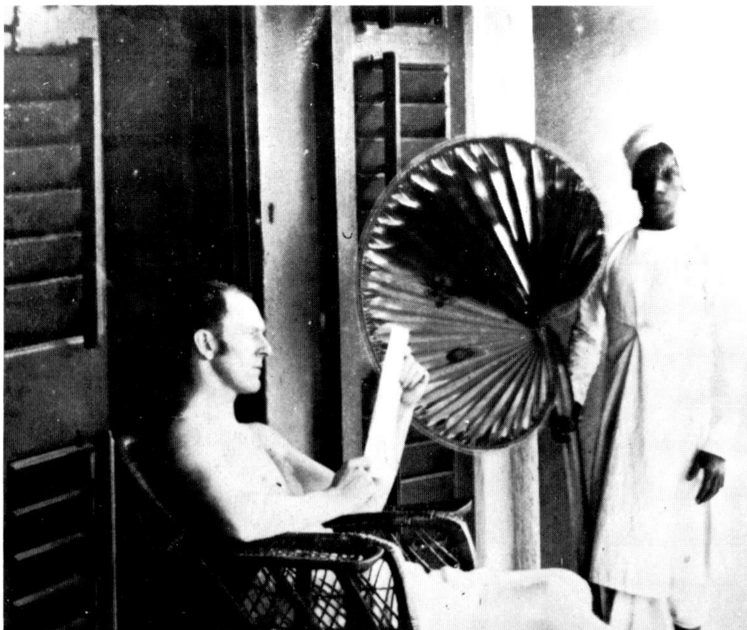

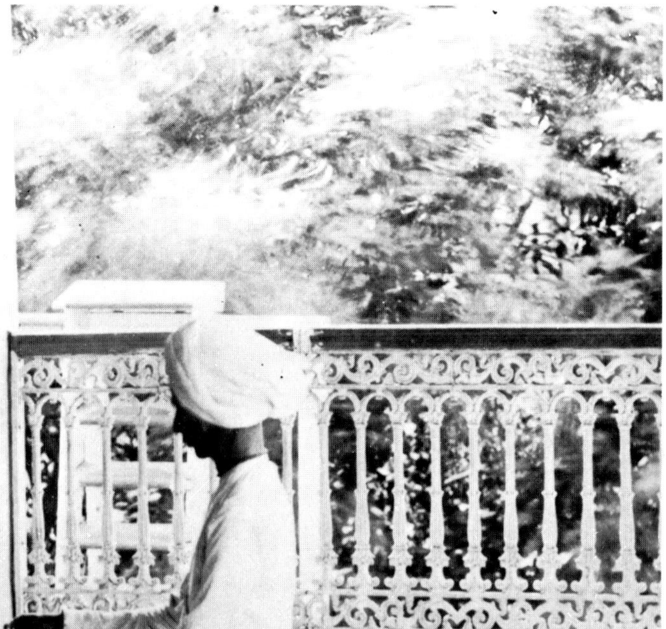

Imperialism gave colonists an elegant lifestyle and British trade flourished; for the natives, life was never to be the same again.

Above left Settlers in Australia with Aborigine slaves, in 1855.

Left A British officer accepts the luxuries of India, *c.*1870.

Above Victorian taste and Imperial grandeur at the Majolica Fountain in the Eastern Dome of the International Exhibition of 1862.

Left Queen Victoria at Balmoral in Scotland, in 1862, with John Brown her favourite 'gilly' (personal servant).

Top British troops on manoeuvre at Port Elizabeth, Cape Province, about 1870.

Above Cavalry embarking at Portsmouth, en route for India, *c.*1900.

A Grenadier officers' mess during the Boer War (1899-1902). The difficulty with which the army suppressed the Dutch colonists in South Africa came as a shock to the British public.

Two sundowners in the Australian outback, *c.*1900.

Two royal babies *c.*1900 – the elder would become Edward VIII, the younger, George VI.

A house party at Abergeldie in Scotland with the Prince of Wales (third from
the left) shortly before his accession to the throne in 1901 as Edward VII.

India was 'the brightest jewel in the British crown' and its importance was formally recognized by royal visits.

Left Pomp and circumstance, Indian style, for Edward VII's coronation durbar at Delhi, in December 1902.

Above George V and Queen Mary arrive at Salingarh Bastion and are escorted to the fort beneath the imperial umbrella, 1911.

The British left their own distinctive imprint on the Empire.

Above A settler's bungalow in India, equipped for tennis.

Above right The doctor's dispensary in Quetta (now in Pakistan) shortly before an earthquake which almost completely destroyed the city in 1935.

Right Bowler hats and hansom cabs in George Street, Sydney, around the turn of the century.

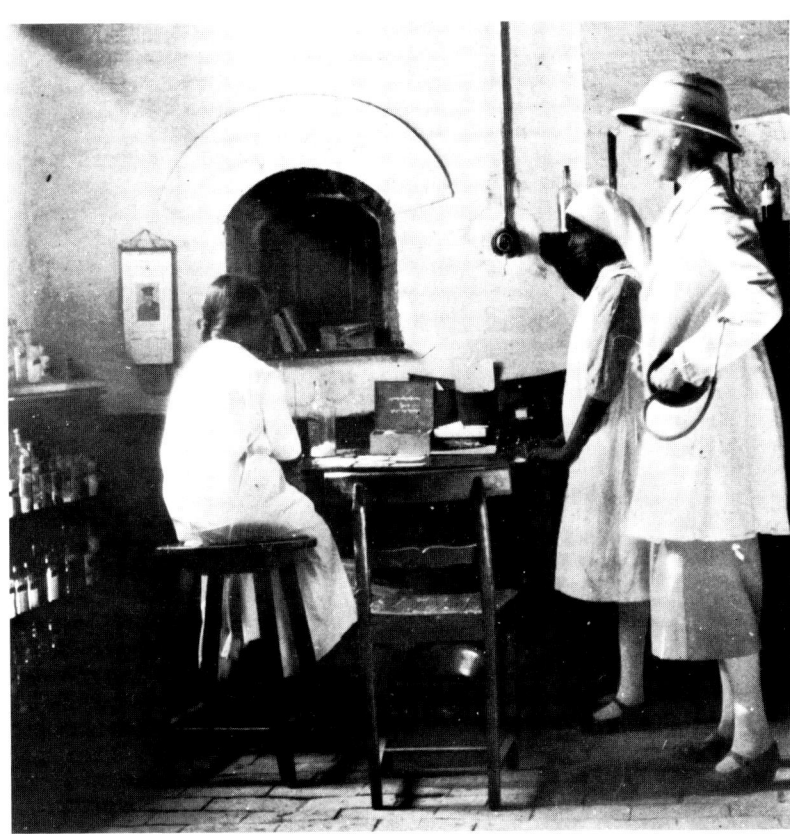

Above The Mile End Road, in London's East End, prepares to greet George VI and Queen Elizabeth (now the Queen Mother) in 1937.

Above right George V and Queen Mary with their grand-daughter, Princess Elizabeth (now Queen Elizabeth II), in 1933.

Right Officers of the Indian Army at Hampton Court in June, 1937 for the coronation of George VI.

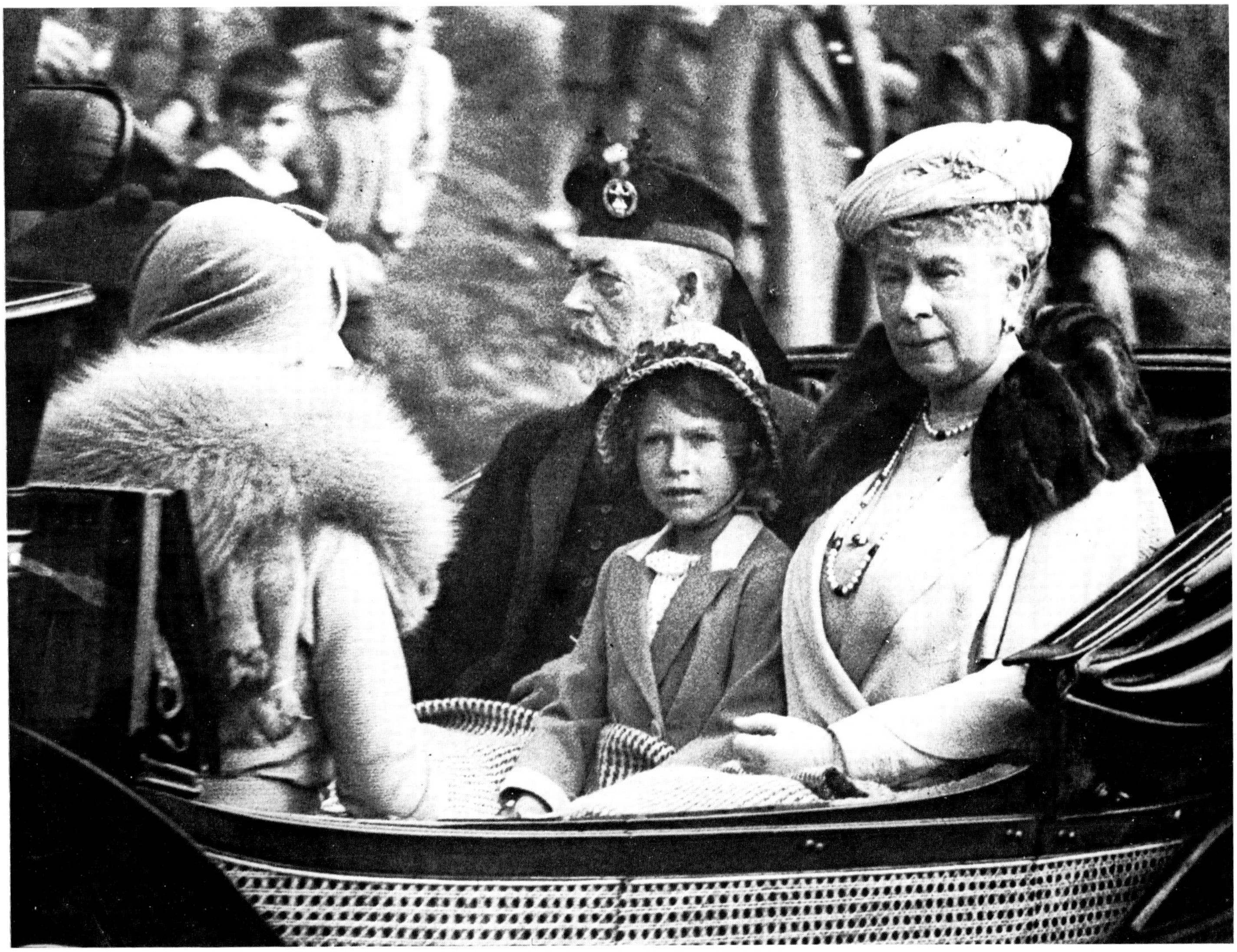

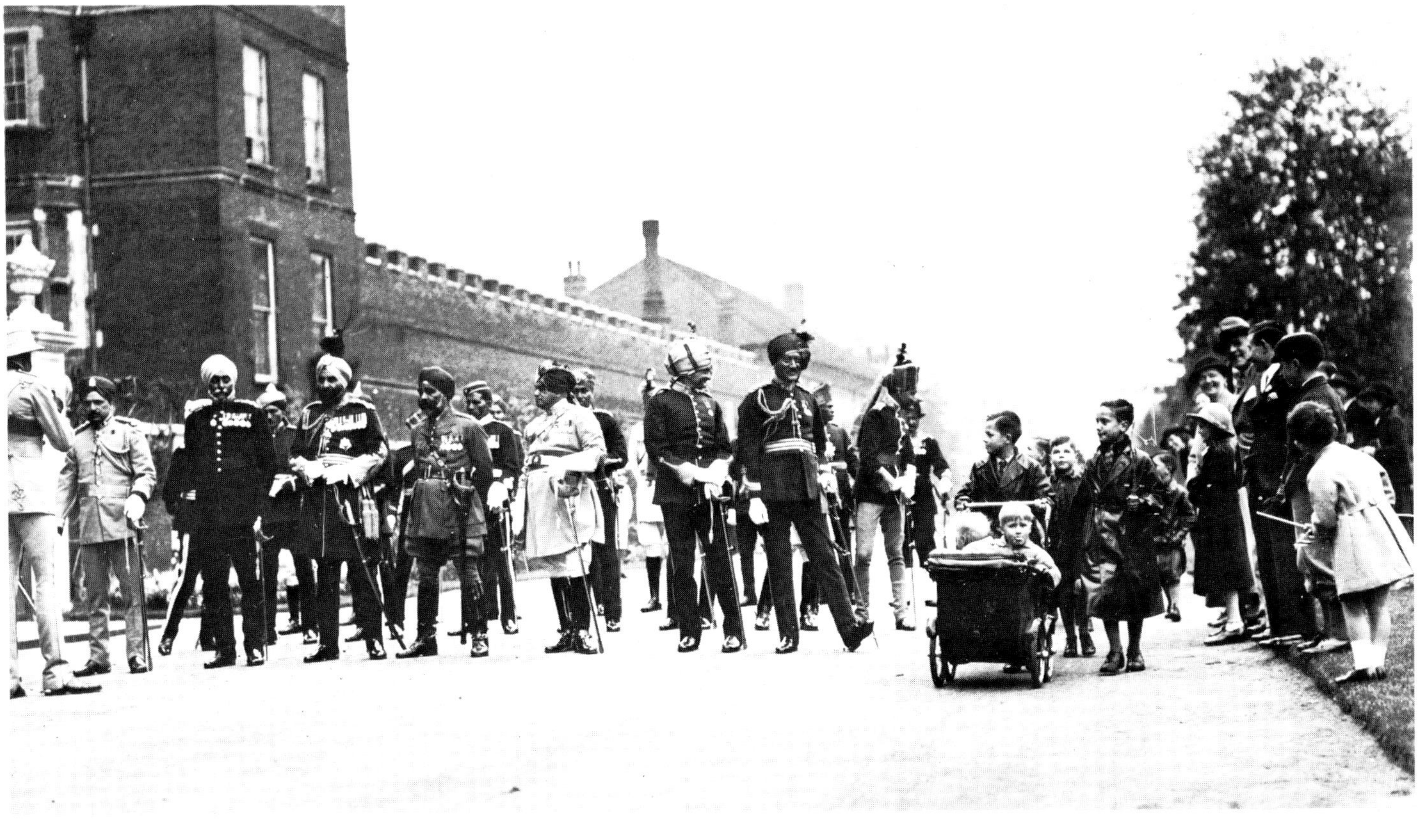

George V at the helm of his yacht, *Britannia,* in 1924.

The Governor of the Tower of London proclaims the new king, Edward VIII, in January 1936. Edward abdicated 10 months later.

George VI took his duties as a monarch very seriously, making every effort to meet his subjects.

Above The Royal Family at the wedding of the Queen's niece, at St. Margaret's Church, Westminster, in 1938.

Left Chatting with tenants during a tour of the Duchy of Cornwall in 1937.

Princess Margaret and Princess
Elizabeth in 1940, knitting comforts
for the troops.

A symbol of Britain's colonial role in 1952 — a district commissioner presides over a native court in the Sudan.

Above A dress rehearsal for the Royal Tournament in 1956 — a reminder of the nation's glorious past.

Left The Coronation of Queen Elizabeth II at Westminster Abbey on June 2nd, 1953. No longer Empress of a third of the world, the Queen is styled merely as Head of the Commonwealth.

Transport

Above Isambard Kingdom Brunel, in front of his steamship the *Great Eastern,* just before his death in 1859.

Right A party of VIPs, including Gladstone, at London's Edgeware Road Station (as it was then spelt) for a trial run of the new underground railway in May 1862.

Most Victorian transport was horse-drawn.

Left A crowded 'Knifeboard' omnibus in London in 1865.

Above A horse-drawn hansom cab of the 1870s.

Above A motor bus on the Glasgow to Tarbet road in the summer of 1909.

Far left Tea clippers in London's East India Docks in 1892.

Left Fishermen and their coracles in Wales in 1856.

Electric trams soon replaced the horse drawn version.

Above Horse tram drivers were exposed to the elements.

Right London's first electric tramway was opened in 1903.

Air travel still seemed quixotic to most people before the 1920s — it was dangerous and, without instruments, flying was possible only on clear days.

Above A Farman triplane in 1908.

Above right Balloons being prepared for the Hurlingham race in the same year.

Right Short's biplane at Eastchurch preparing for a transatlantic flight in 1919.

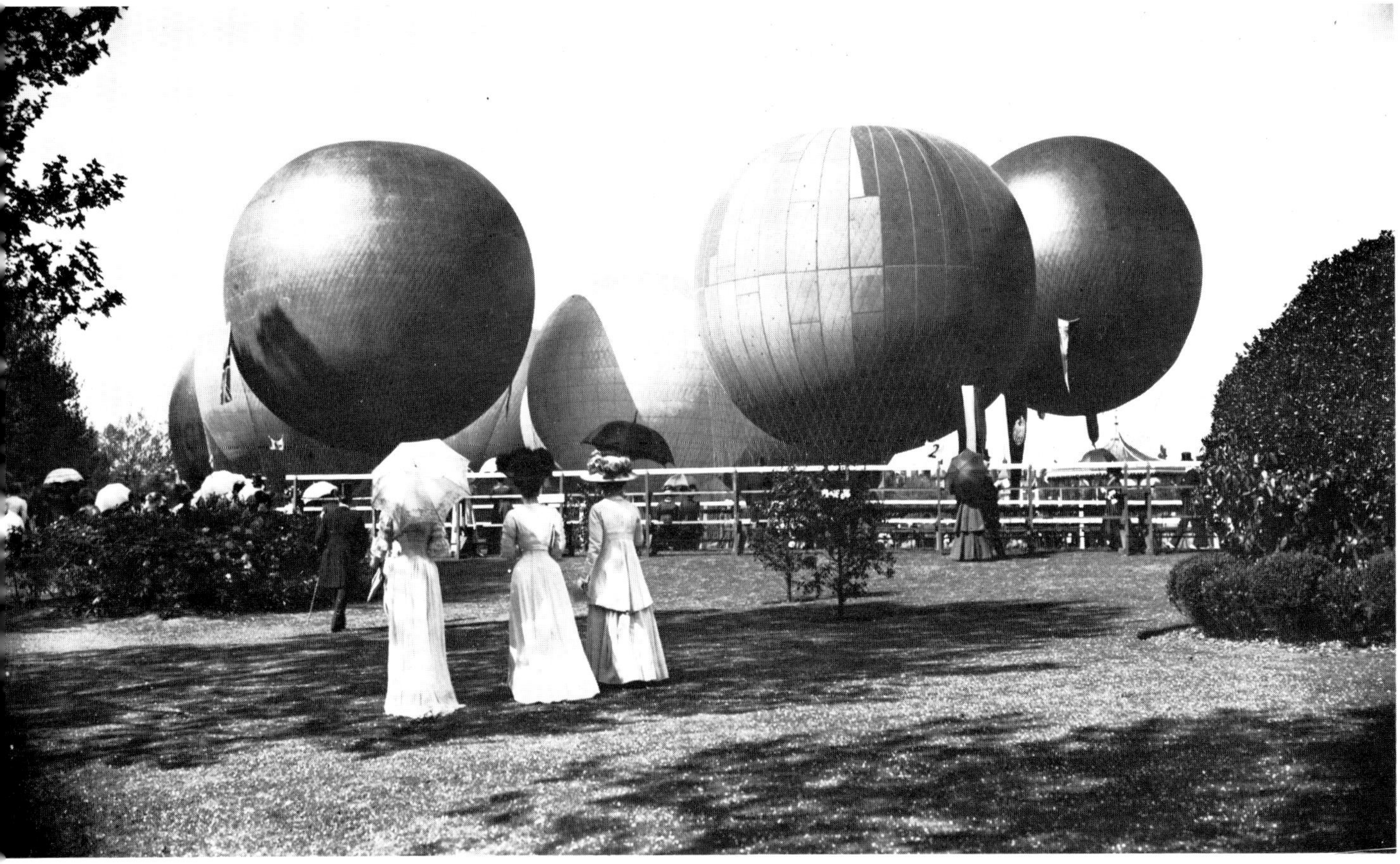

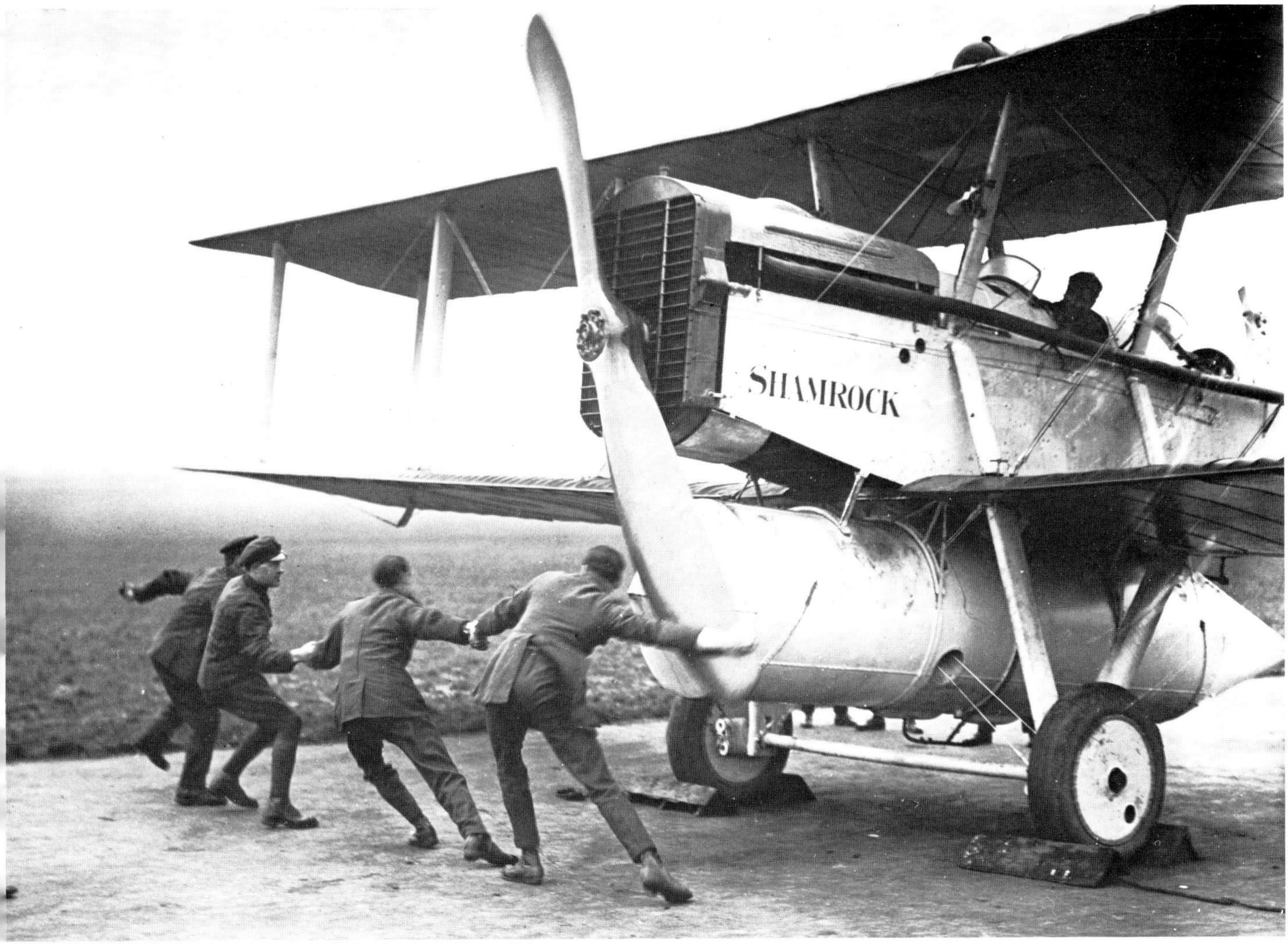
SHAMROCK

Top Ocean liner *Mauretania* on her maiden voyage from Liverpool in November 1907.

Top right By the 1930s private cars had become common, but there were still steam engines on the road. This one is hauling a 22-ton barge through Hertfordshire.

Above Integrated transport at the Albert Dock and Riverside Quay in Hull, Yorkshire.

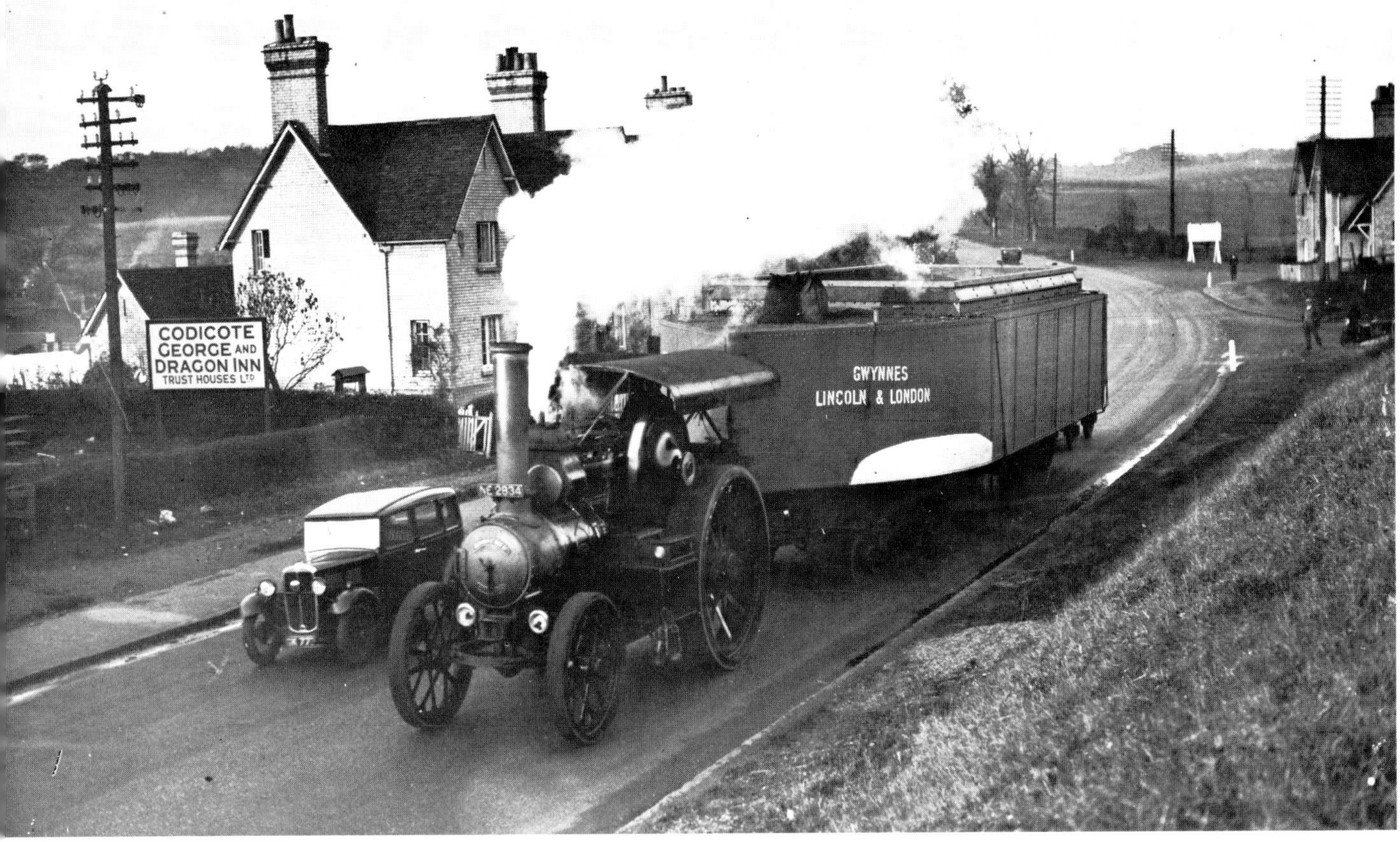
CODICOTE
GEORGE AND
DRAGON INN
TRUST HOUSES LTD
GWYNNES
LINCOLN & LONDON

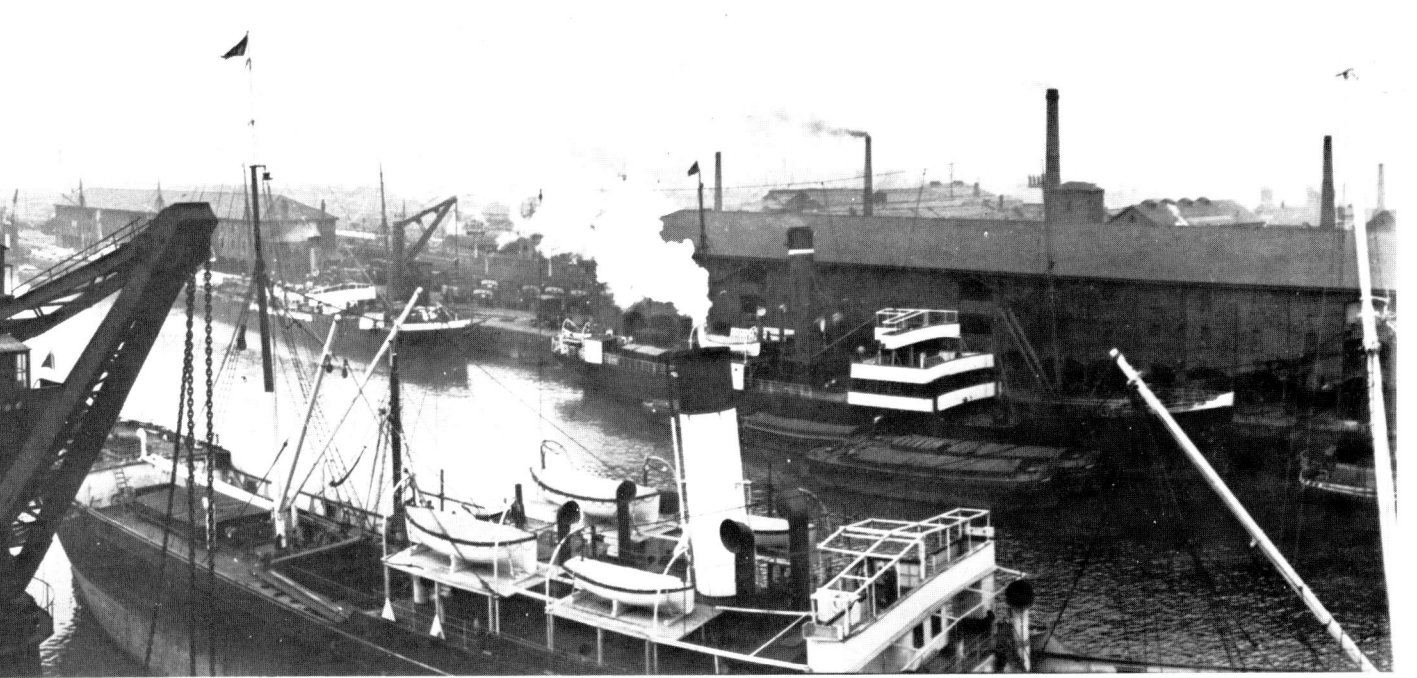

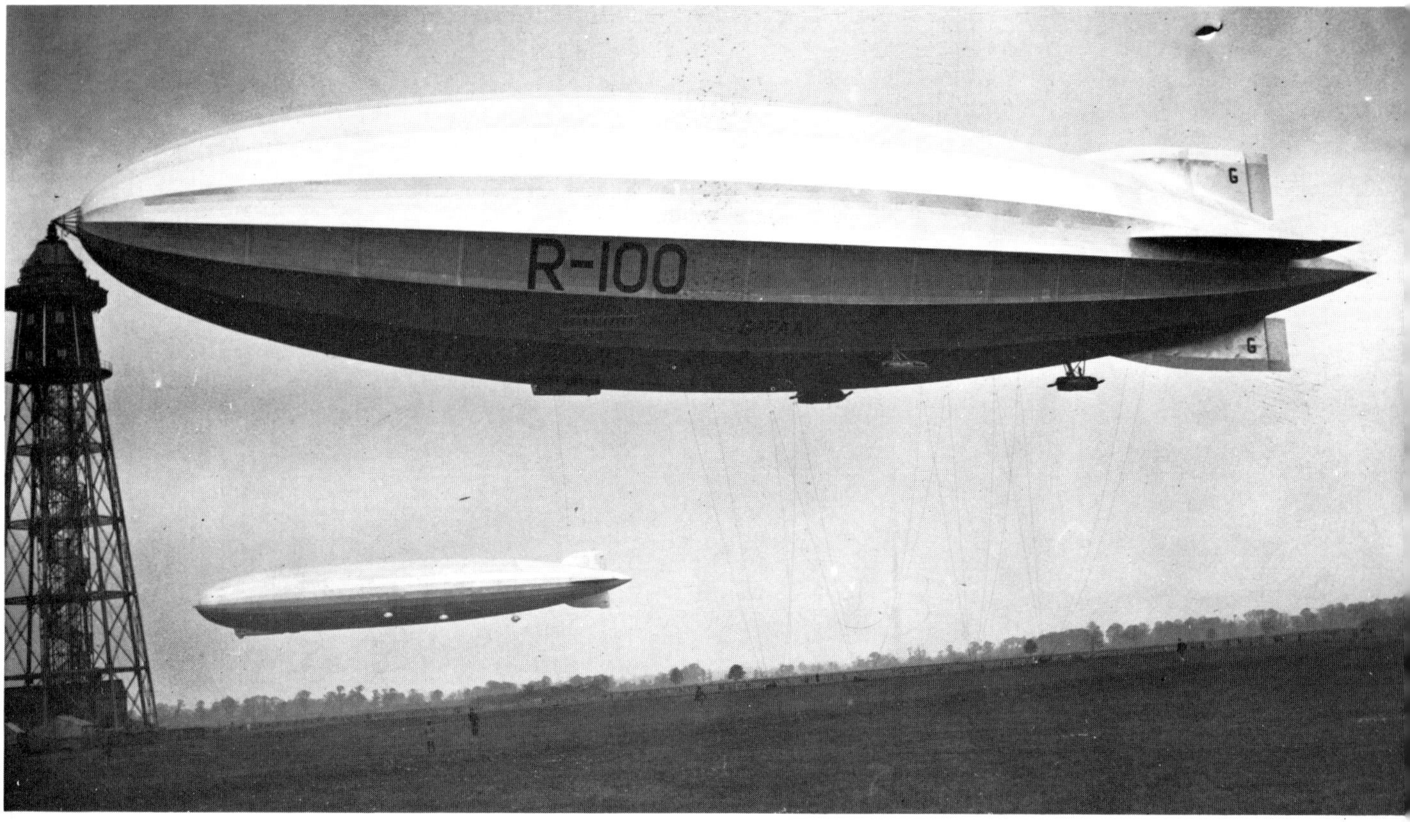
R-100
G
G

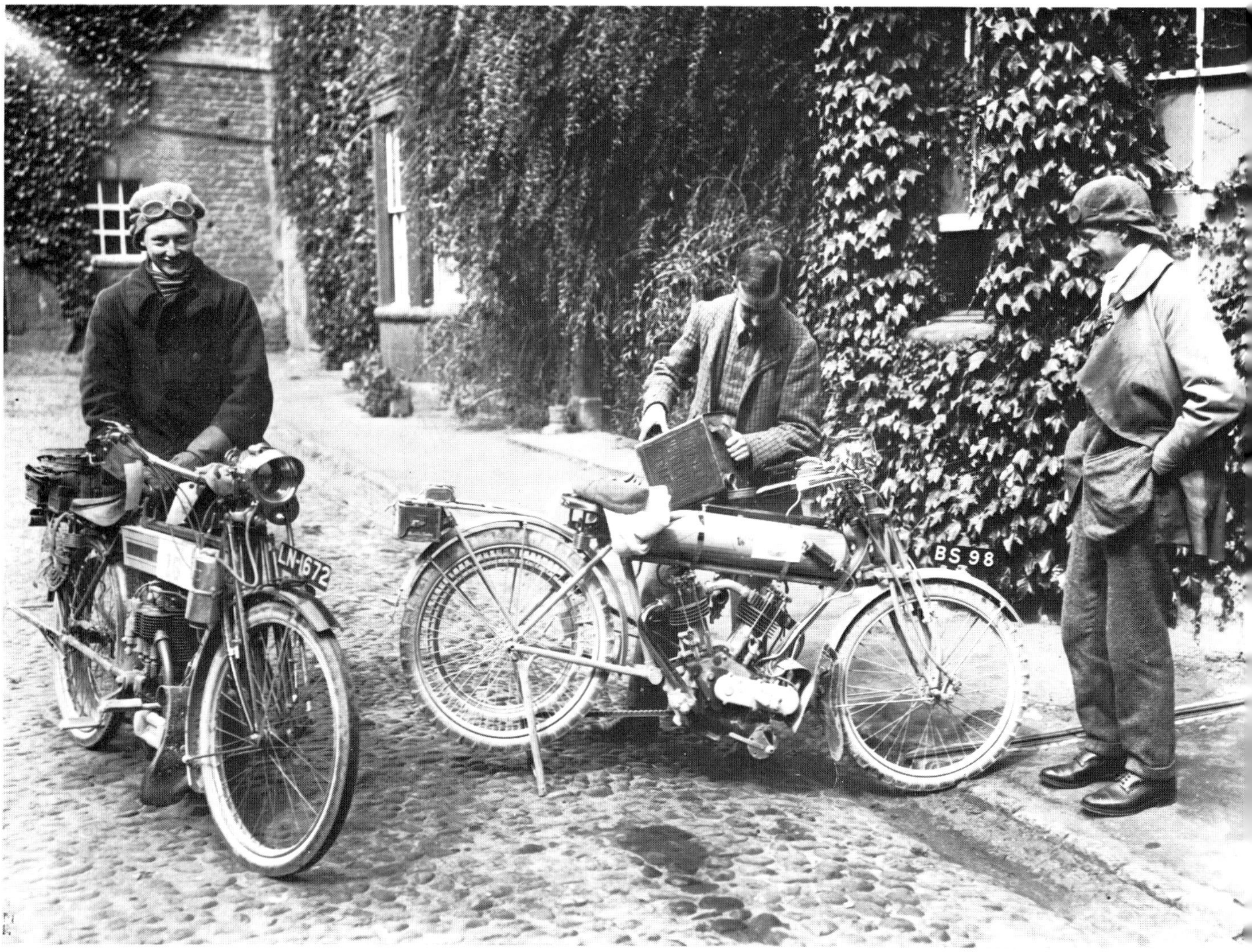
LN-1672
BS 98

Above left The *Graf Zeppelin* arrives at Cardington in April 1930. In the foreground is moored the *R100*. In the same year the *R101* burnt up on the way to India and ended the short career of the British airship.

Left August 1910, motorcyclists filling their tanks at the George Hotel Yard in Stamford.

Above Amy Johnson in November 1932 preparing for her historic flight to South Africa which took her a mere four days and six hours.

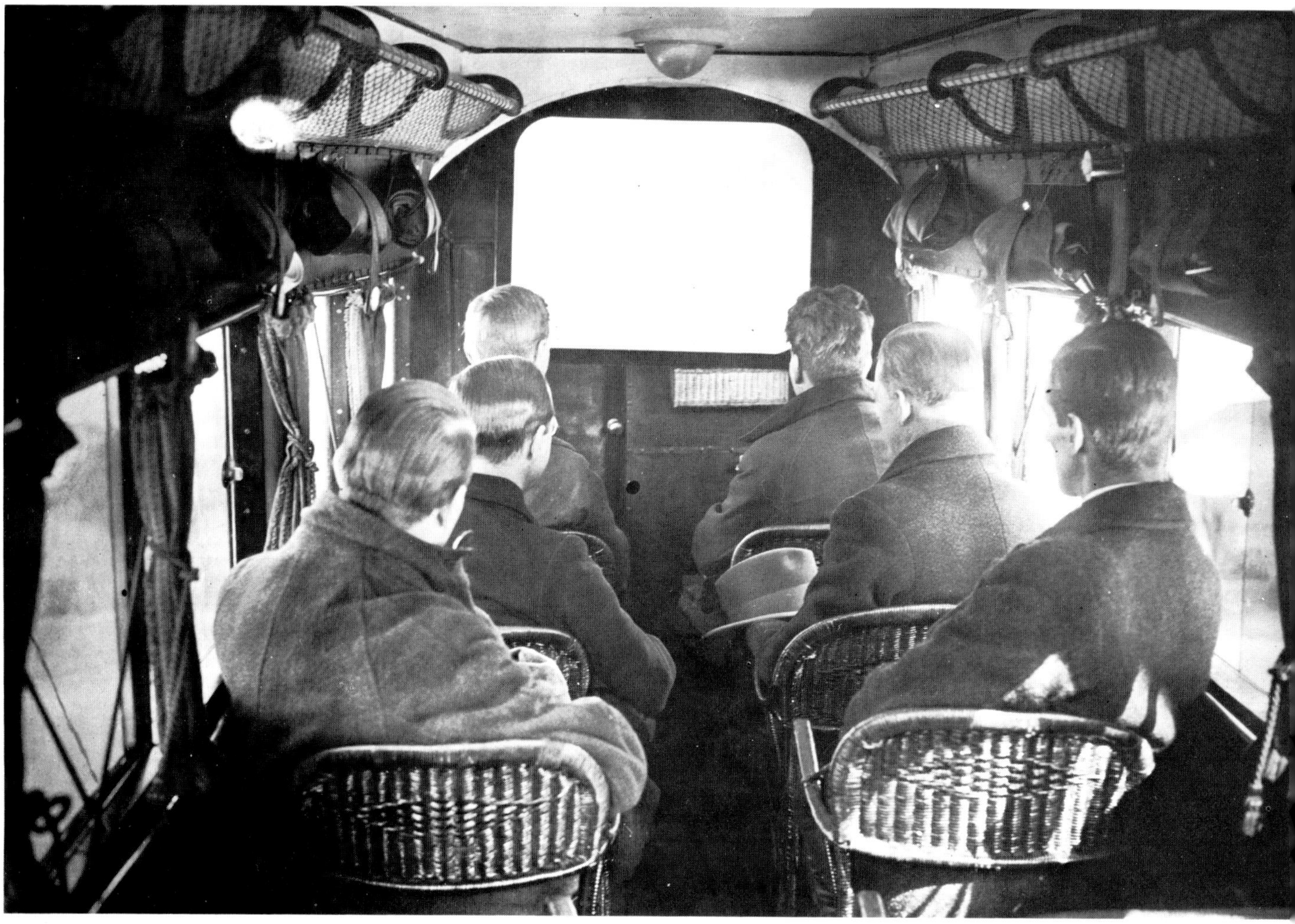

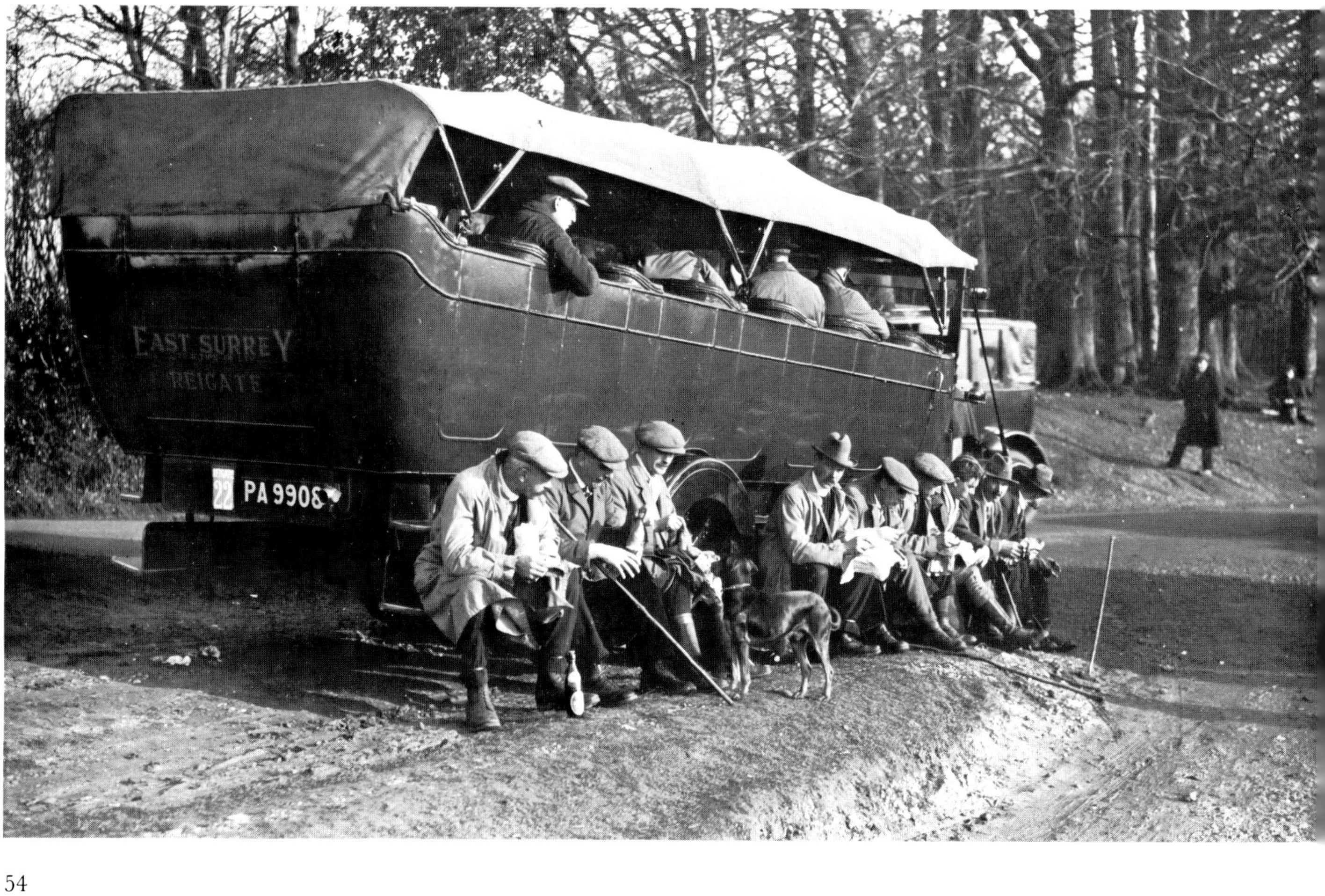
EAST SURREY
REIGATE
PA 9908

Top left The first cinema show in an airliner in 1925 — there were few other comforts.

Left December 1926, a charabanc near Newlands Corner in Surrey. The passengers were not on a day trip, they were policemen searching for a murder victim.

Above A barge in one of London's canals in 1954 — road and rail transport had already taken away most of the traffic from England's canals.

Above Christmas Eve, 1932, a special holiday train leaves London's Euston Station for the North.

Above right Hurrying home from a Manchester factory, 1938.

Right Victoria Station, London, on August Bank Holiday, 1936.

"SIMO" TYRESOLES
TYRESOLES
100% NEW TYRE MILEAGE
AT HALF THE COST
WALKDEN

NEWS THEATRE
TRUTH WELL TOLD
MORNING POST
T.M. SUTTON

Above Commuters preparing to leave for London in 1946.

Above right Personal mobility with a motor scooter, 1954.

Industry

Britain's lead in industry had made her the workshop of the world by 1856, exporting machinery as well as manufactured goods.

Above Bricks for building.

Right The Penn and Sons works in Deptford, building steamships in the 1860s.

Above Masts for the sailing ships, 1863.

Left The herring catch at Lowestoft fish market, 1870.

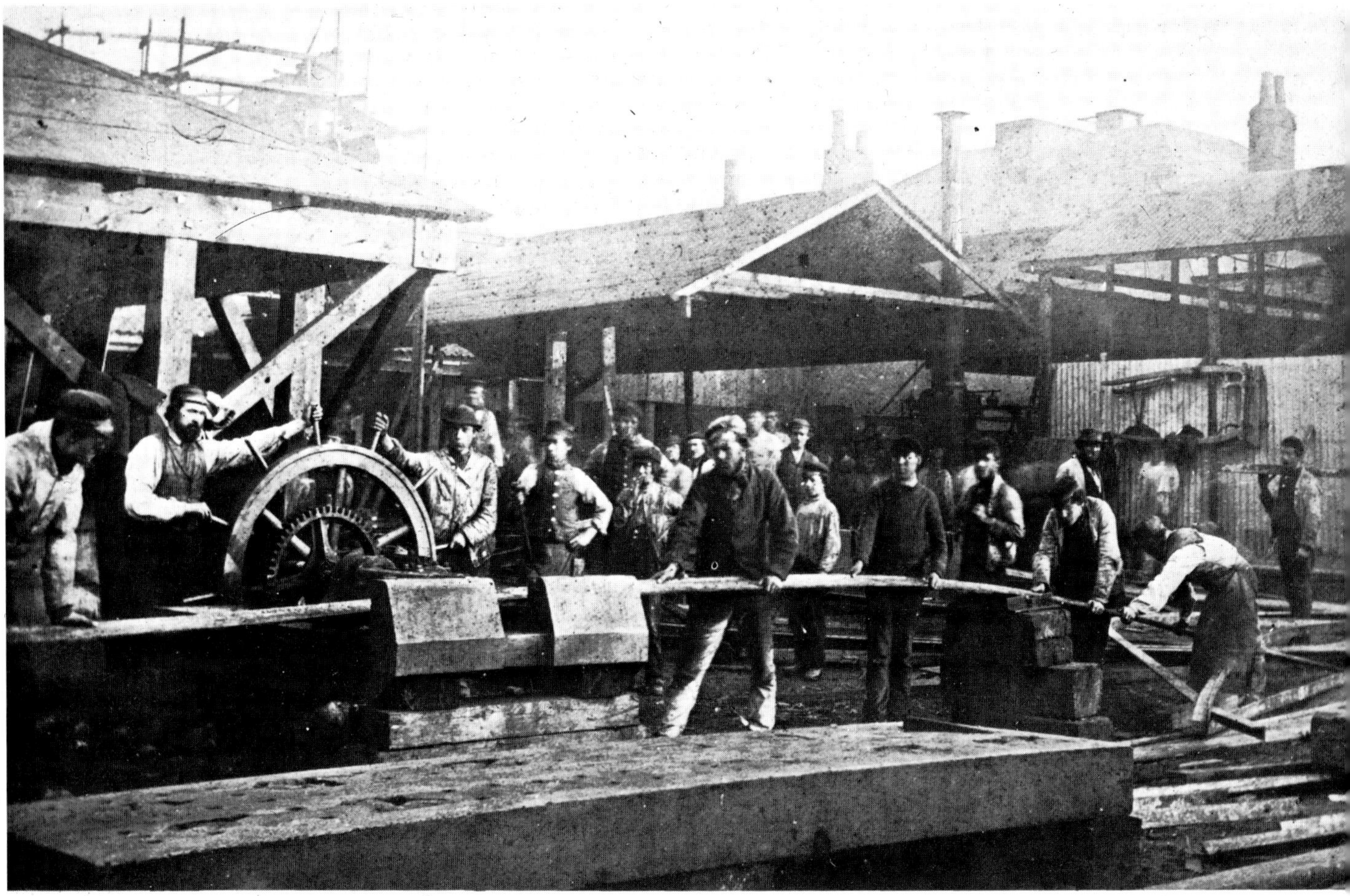

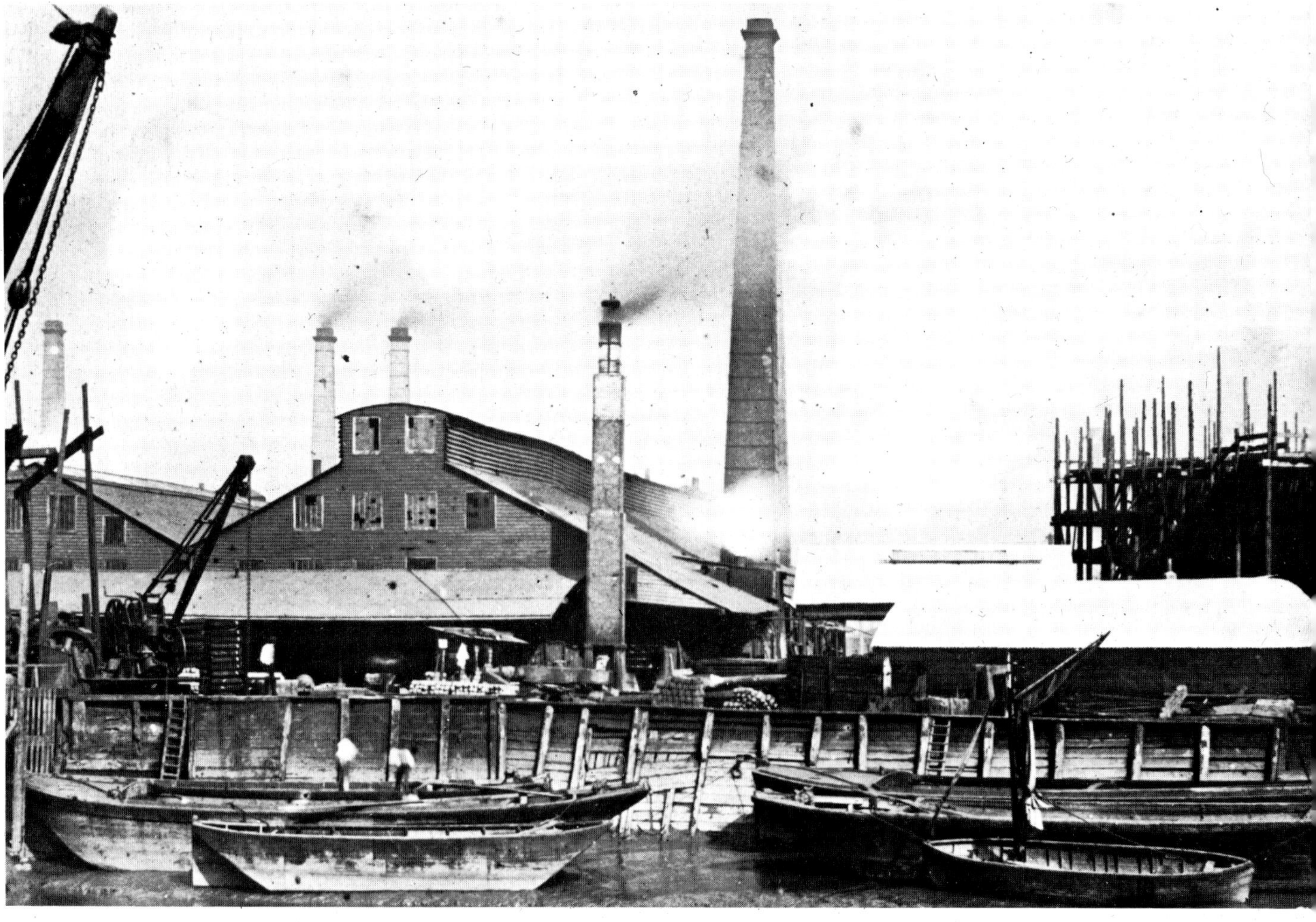

Heavy industry was based entirely on iron until the development of steelmaking techniques in the 1850s.

Above An engineering works, in 1867, where pig iron was recast for machinery.

Above left and left Iron foundries in the 1860s where crude ores were converted to bar and plate.

Child labour, *c*.1908. Most children left school at the age of twelve.

Above Loading shells at the Vickers armaments factory in 1915. During the
First World War many women were employed in heavy industry for the first
time.

Above right Women workers at the Jacob biscuit factory in Liverpool labelling
tins on an early conveyor belt, *c.*1925.

Right Dyed cloths at Eastmans Laundry, 1910.

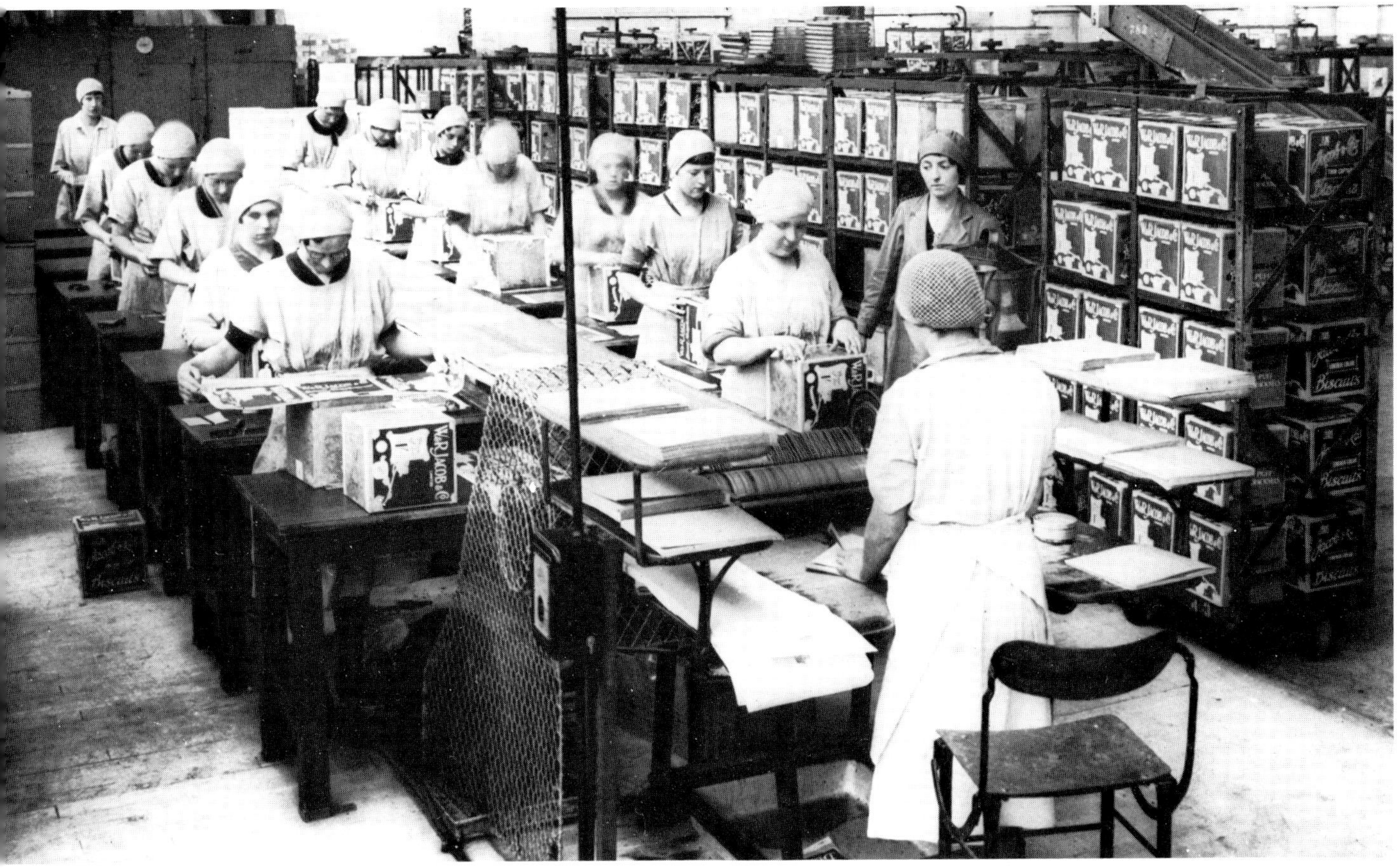
Biscuits

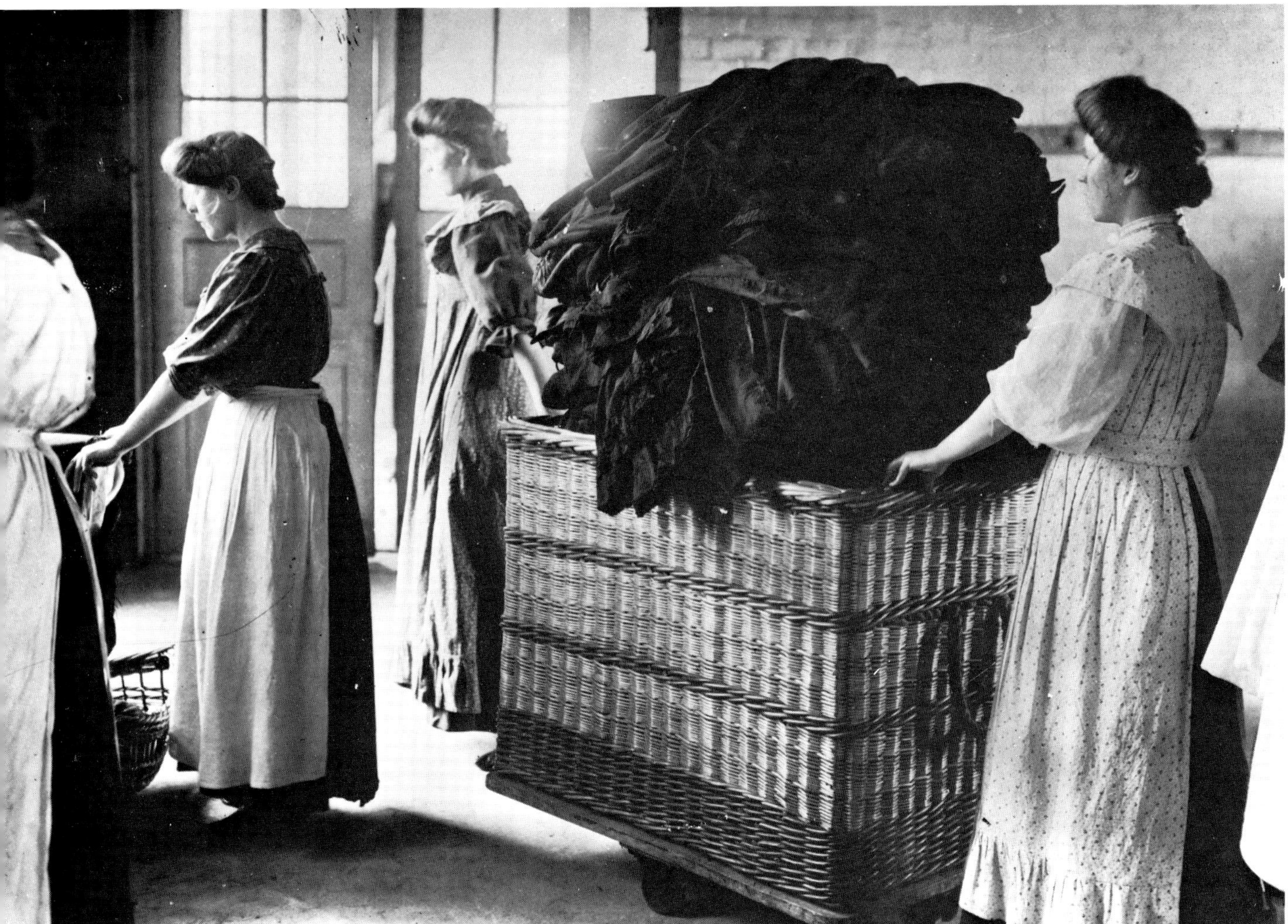

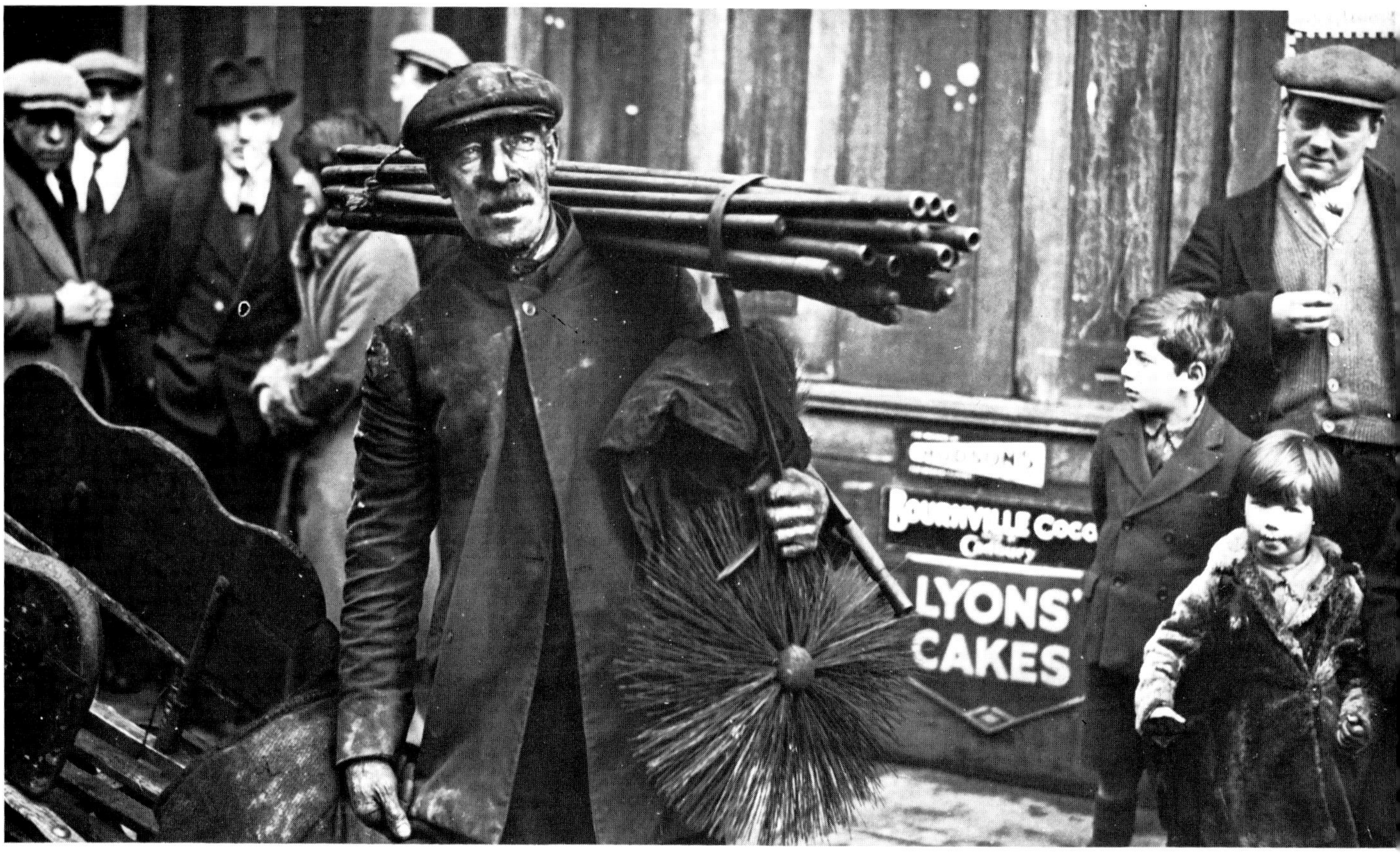
LYONS'
CAKES

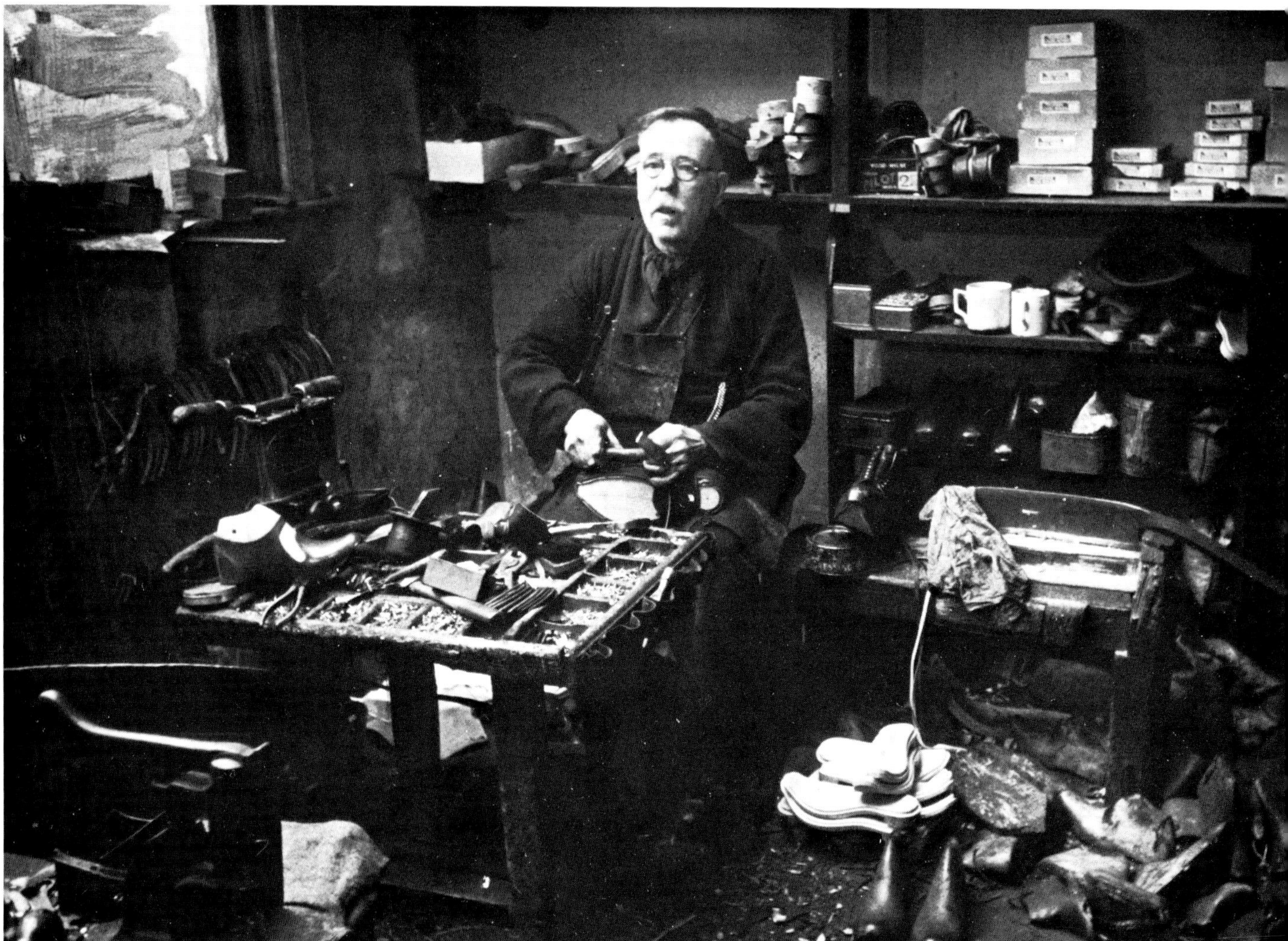

Top left A chimney sweep at Bethnal Green, East London, who also happened to be the mayor in 1931.

Left Carving clogs for miners in Wigan, 1939.

Above Ratcatchers employed by the railways, 1941.

Top left Testing vacuum cleaners at the Electrolux factory in Bedfordshire, 1932. Mass production techniques had revolutionised light industry in Britain.

Left The MG factory at Abingdon in 1932, producing Midgets individually.

Above Face workers at Ellington Colliery, Northumberland, 1951. Coal was still the main source of power.

Above Blast furnaces, steel mills and railway sidings in Sheffield, 1950.

Right Construction work on the Dome of Discovery for the Festival of Britain exhibition in 1951.

Agriculture

Above Butter made on the farm in wooden churns, in 1857.

Right A golden harvest in the Westmorland Dales in the early 1900s.

Westmorland farmhands around the turn of the century. Many were leaving the countryside to find work in the towns.

Above Coming home from the Norfolk marshes, 1887.

Above right Horncastle horsefair in Lincolnshire, 1880.

Right Filling water butts at the village pond, 1905.

81

Sheepfarming in the early
1900s — the wool and meat
still fetched high prices.

Above Shire horses with the plough in 1908.

Above right Early mechanization, as the steam tractor replaces the horses, 1922.

Right The reaping machine replaces the scythe.

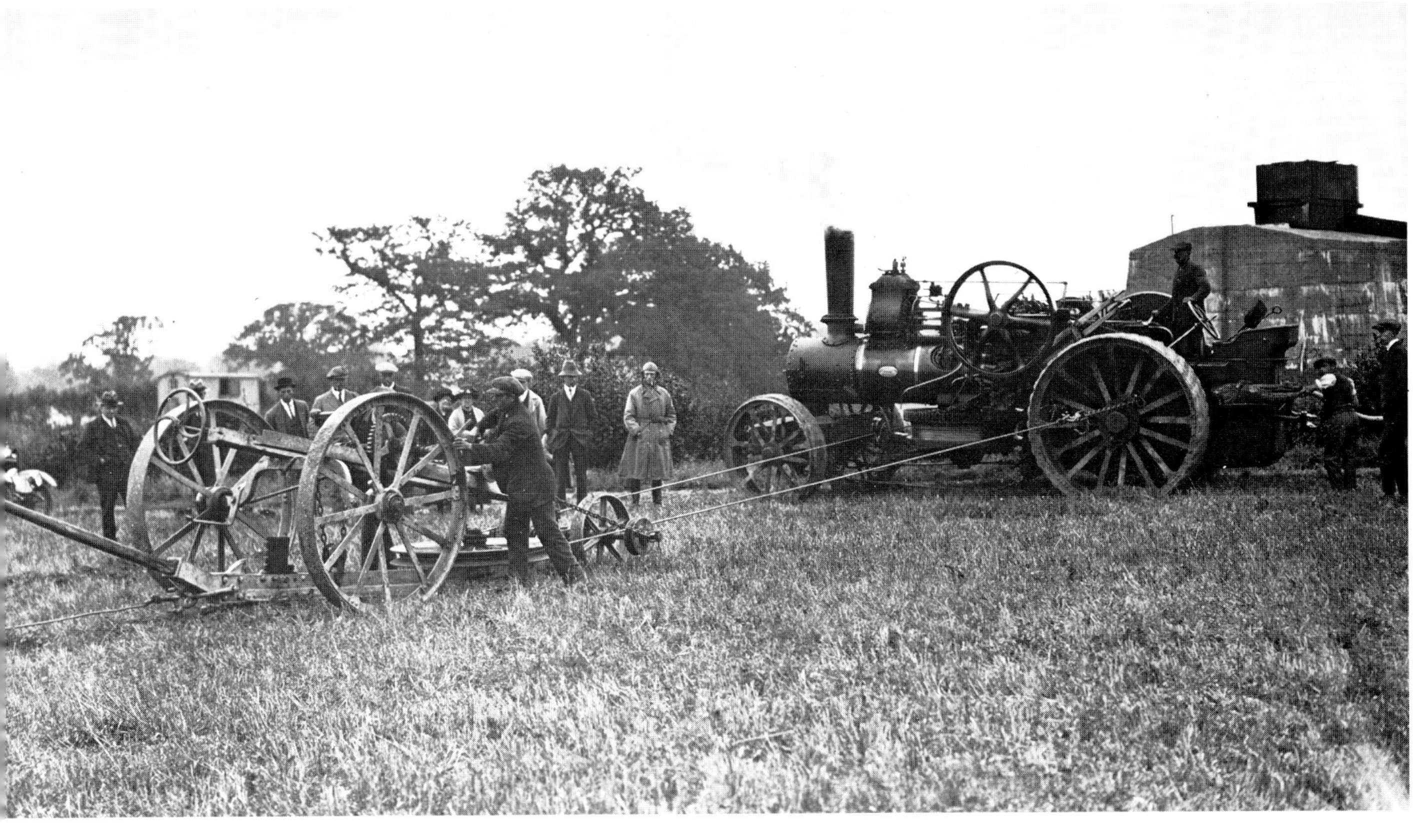

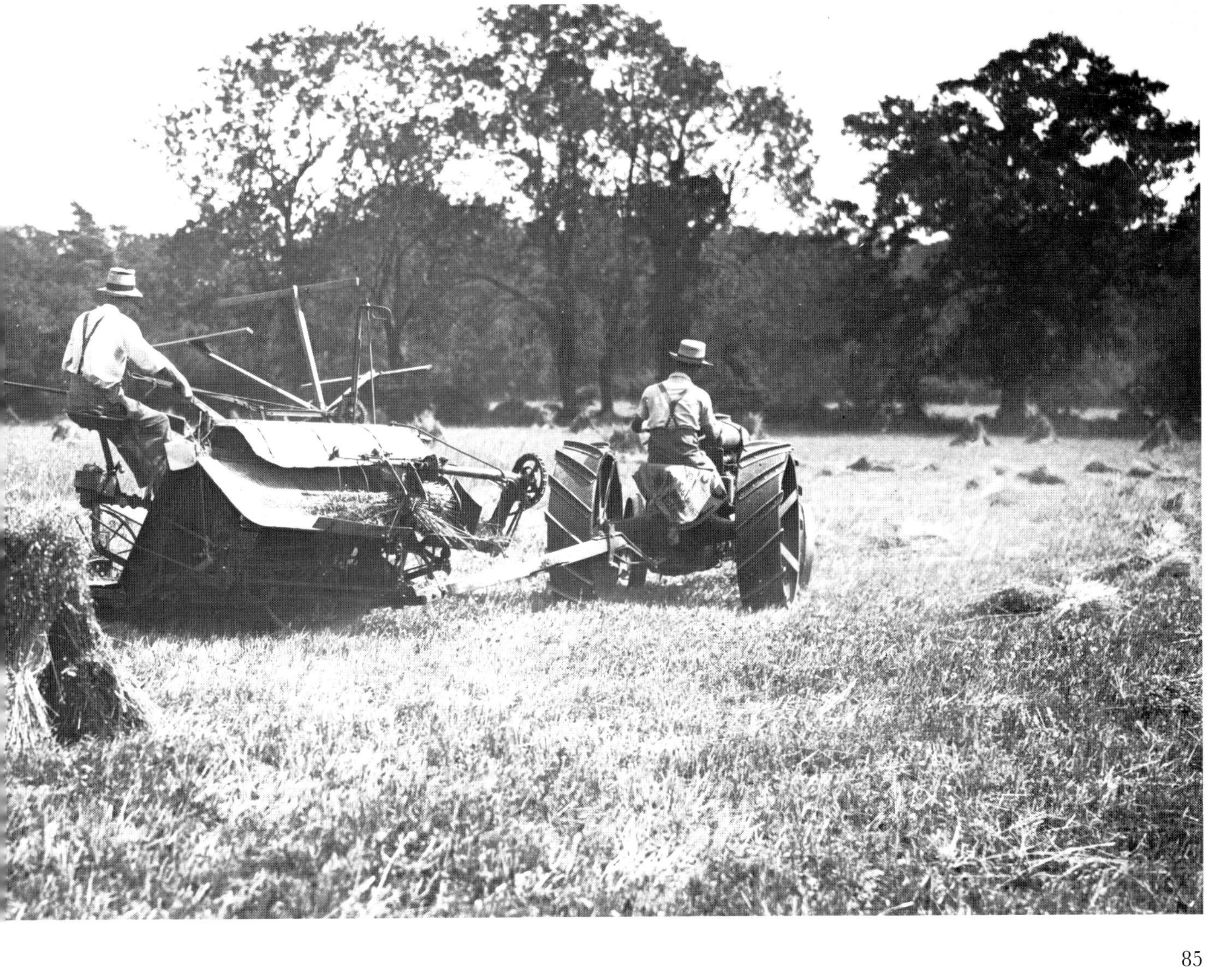

Above A postman delivers to the Cambridge Agricultural Show, July 1922.

Above right Judging cattle at a 1922 dairy competition.

Right Flower stalls at Covent Garden market, London, in 1925.

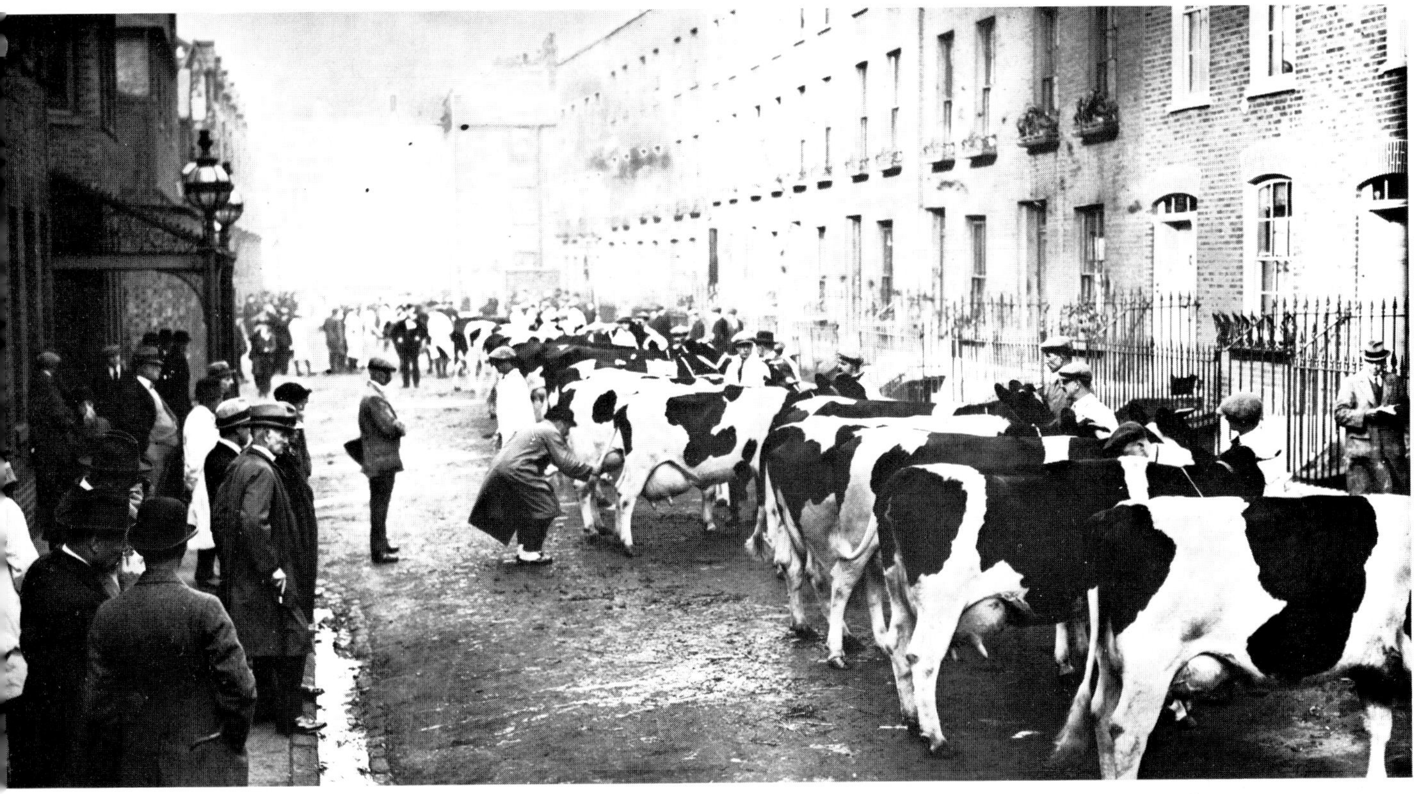

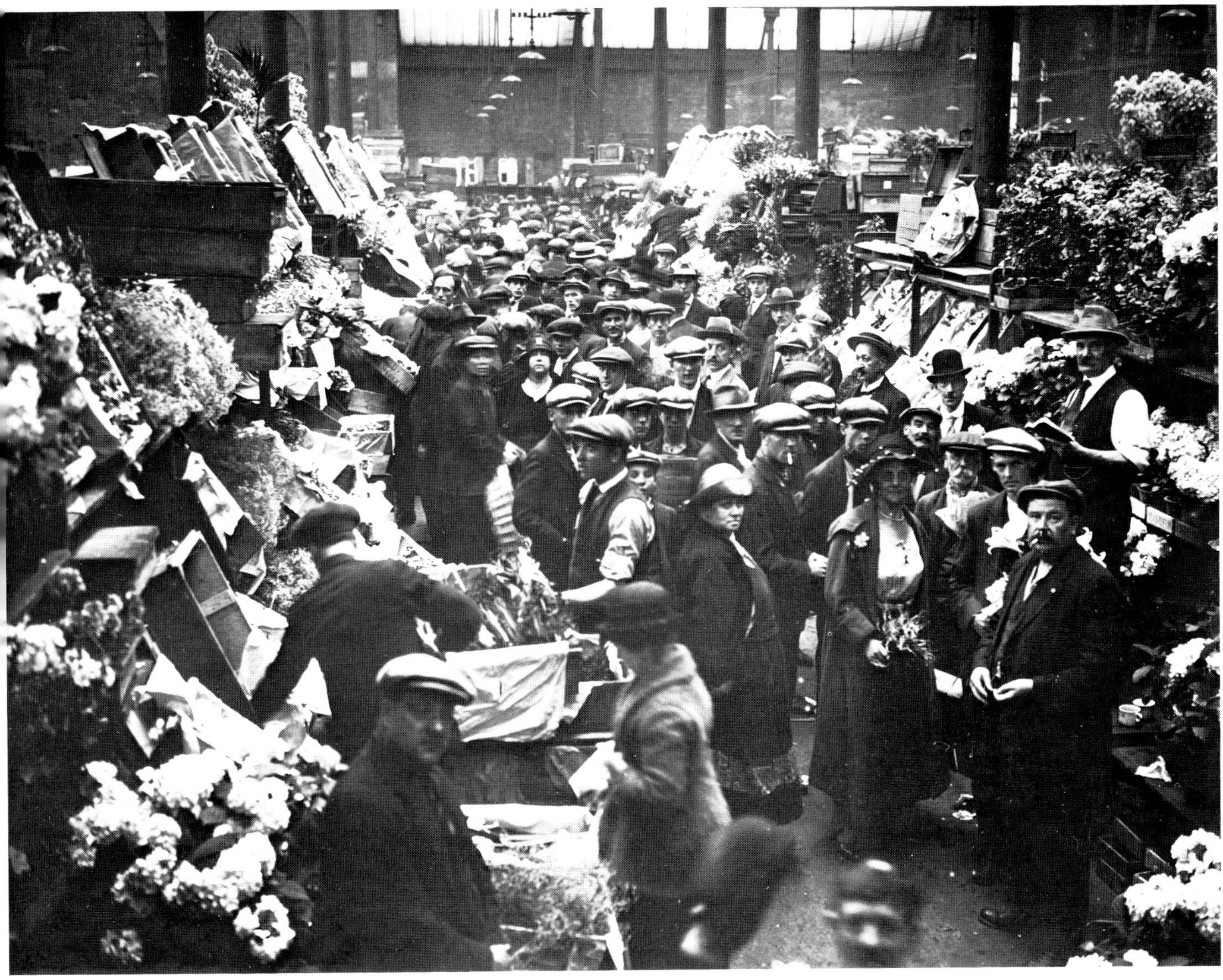

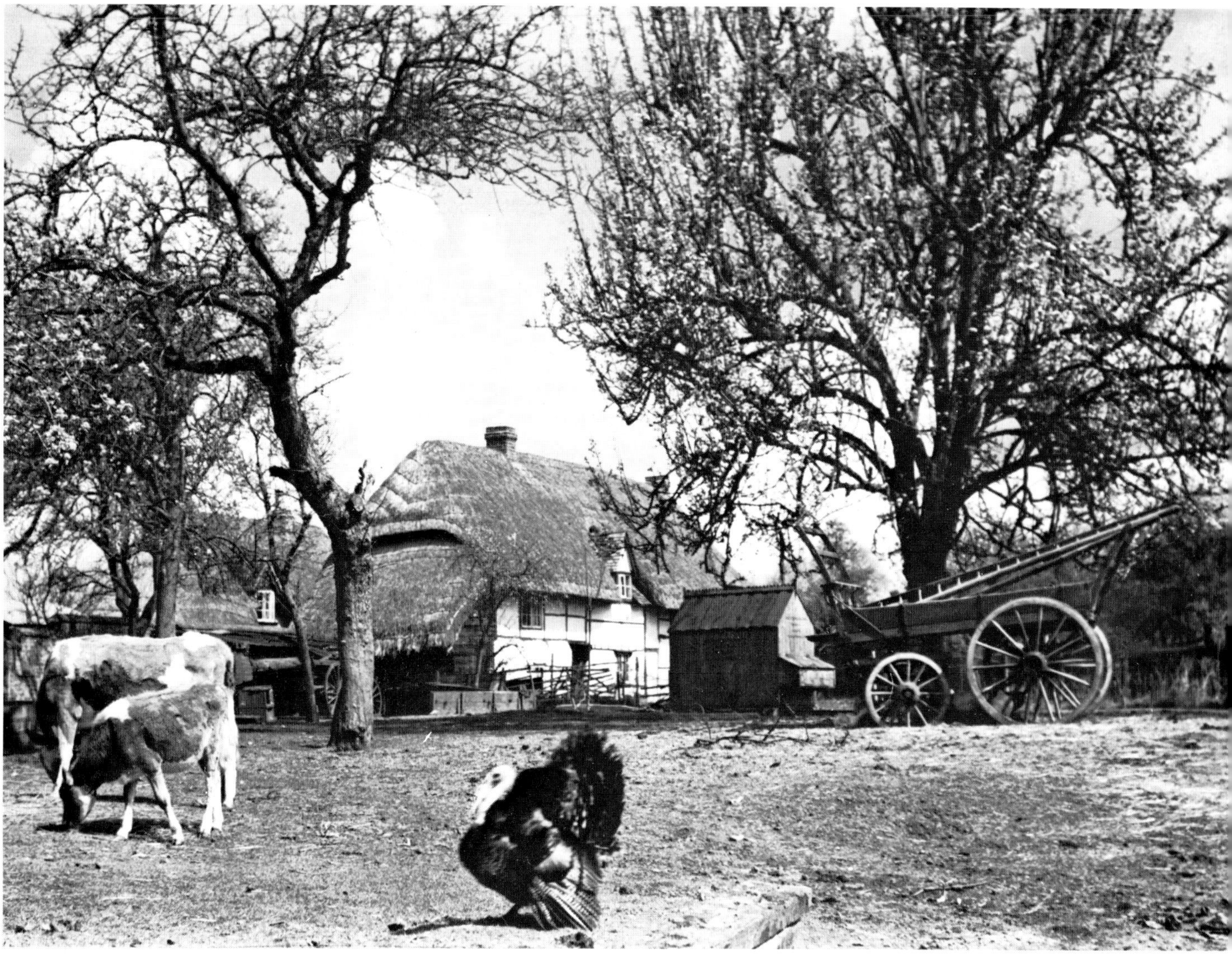

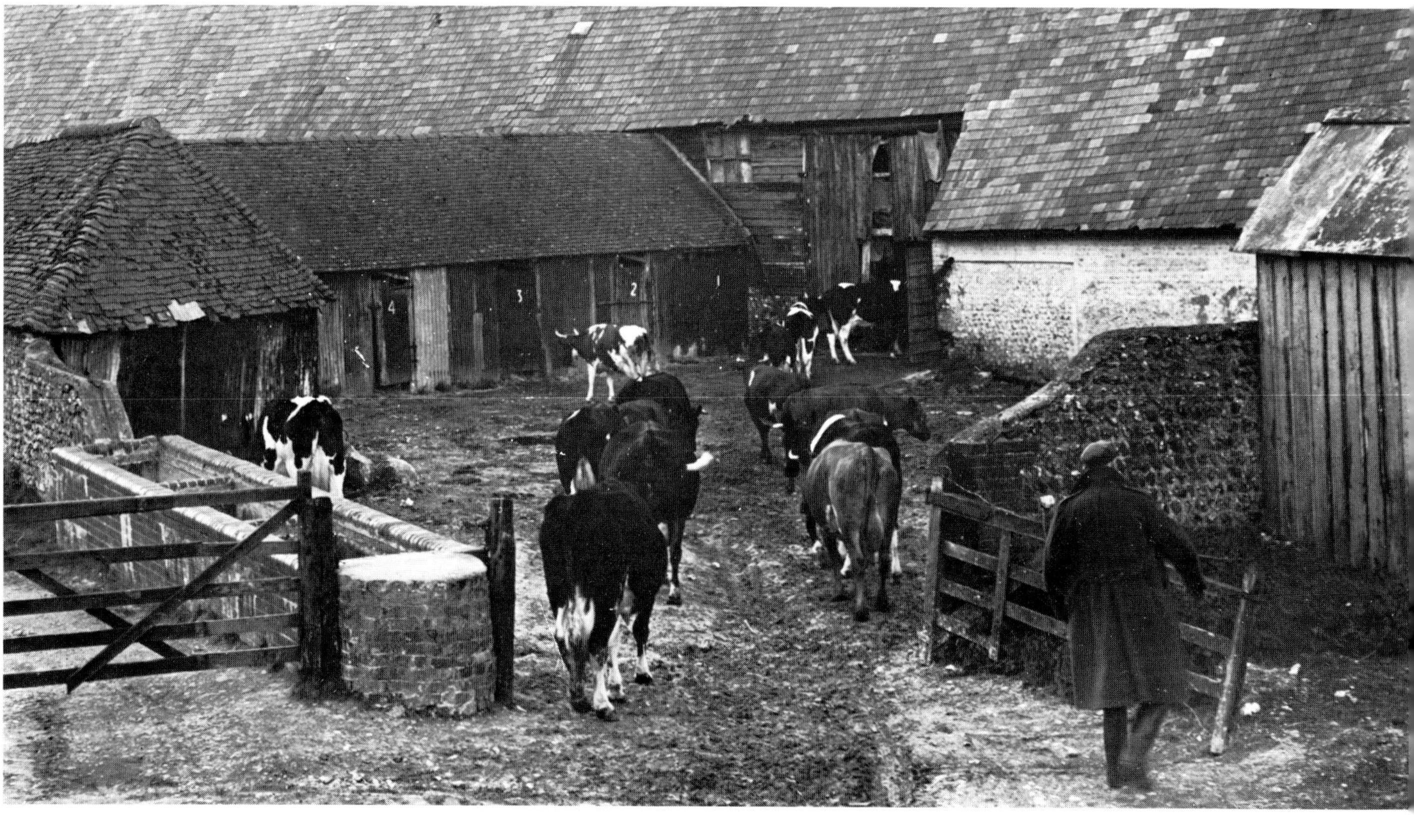

Above left Farmyard springtime at East Hagbourne in Berkshire.

Above Market-gardening at Falmer, near Brighton, 1951.

Left An old tithe-barn, 1954, Patcham Farm, Sussex.

Dairy farmers in the 1950s survived with the help of subsidies from the Milk Marketing Board.

Above A Somerset dairy farmer in 1956.

Left The cattle market at Clitheroe in Lancashire, 1955.

Leisure

Before the 1880s photography was an expensive hobby for a few enthusiasts, but technical advances heralded a golden age for the commercial cameraman.

Above Two fishermen, from Grundy's English Views, taken in 1857.

Right Posing for portraits on Clapham Common, 1877.

British tourists brave the Chamonix glacier in the Alps in 1867. 'Travelling' was a long established pastime of the aristocracy; now the affluent middle-class began to discover its delights.

Above Bicycling in the 1890s.

Right Outside a London pub in the 1870s.

Above Freshwater Bay in the Isle of Wight with boats and bathing machines.

Left The seaside without the sun in the 1890s. With cheap rail transport, more and more people were visiting the coast.

Above An Edwardian maidservant sneaks a game of croquet, 1910.

Right Skating in the same year. Skating rinks transformed a vigorous outdoor sport into a graceful and very popular diversion for city dwellers.

The gentleman's picnic — luncheon beside the Rolls at Royal Ascot in June 1921.

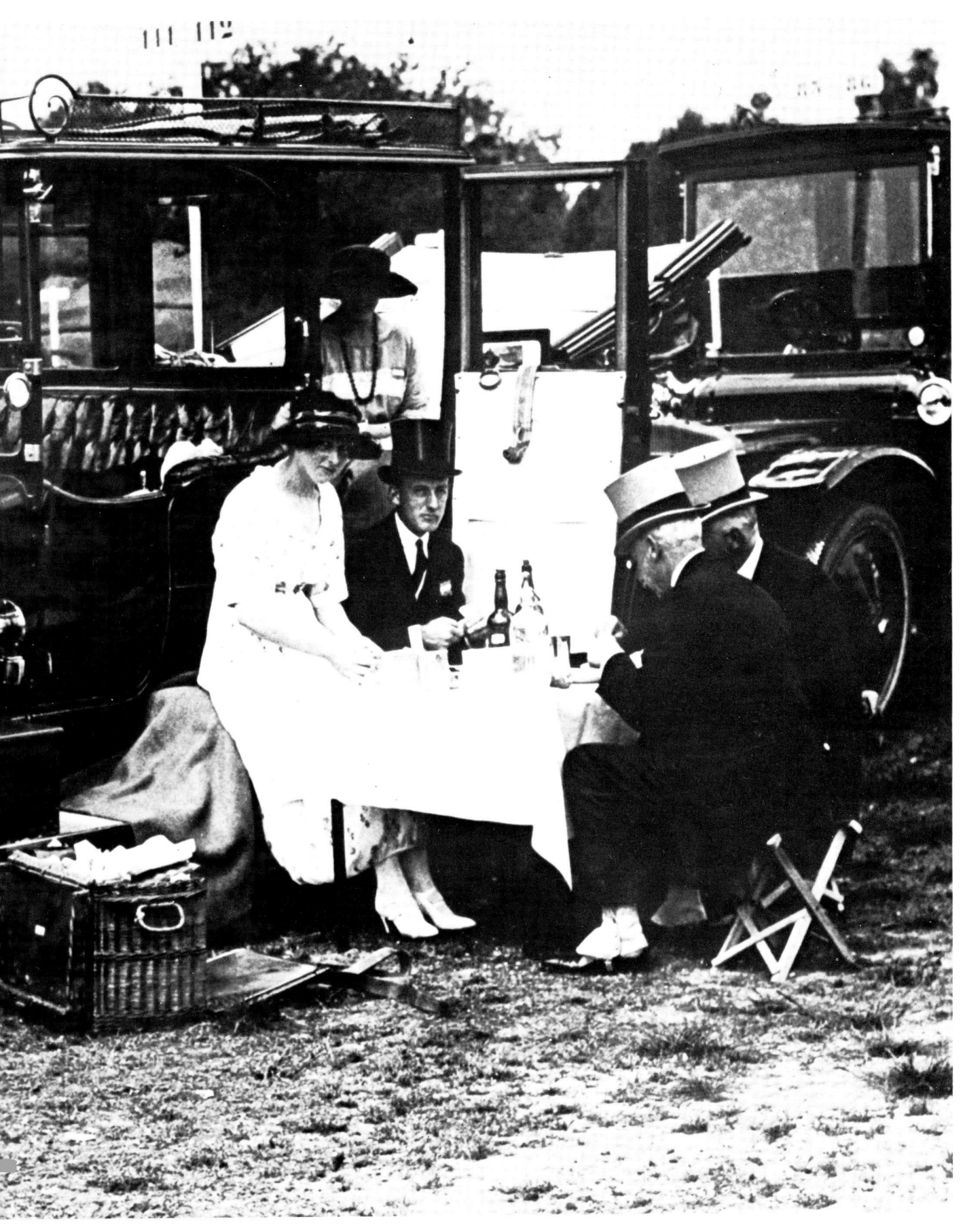

Top left The National Game in January 1913 — West Ham playing against West Bromwich Albion.

Left A boxing tournament at Bodmin in Cornwall in 1922. Like football, boxing became enormously popular between the wars.

Above The patient angler at Egham in Surrey, 1930.

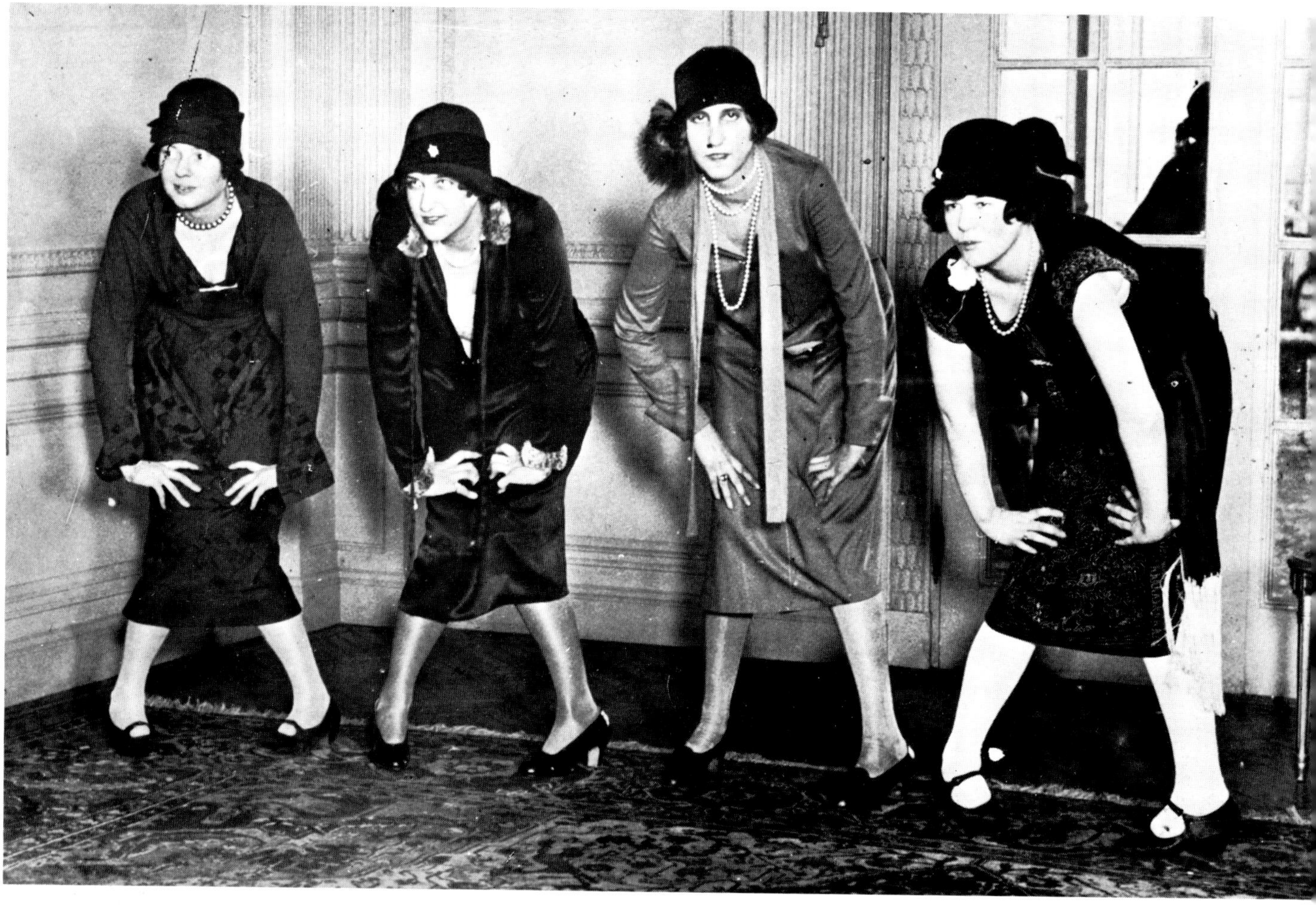

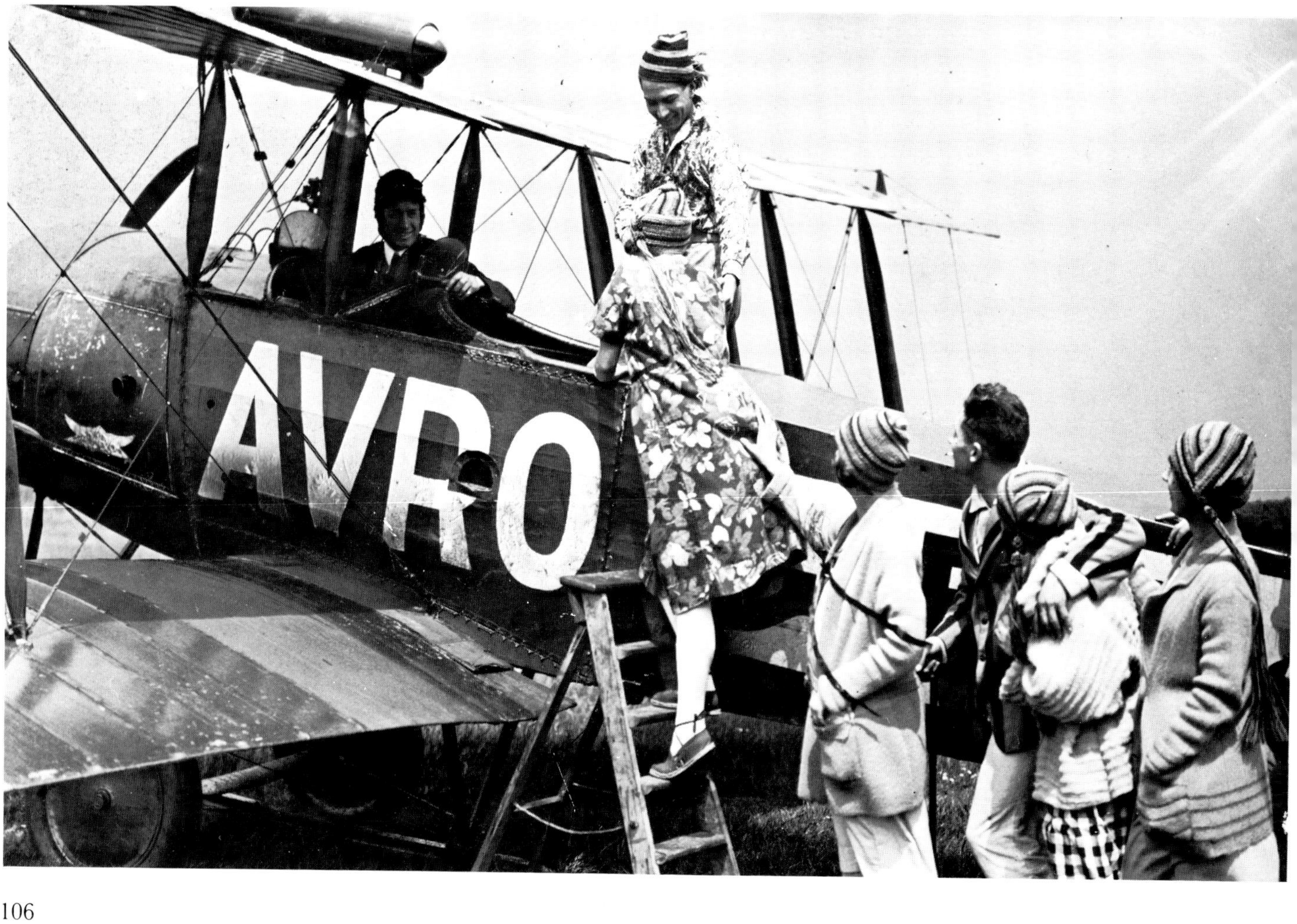
AVRO

Above left and left Two crazes of the 1920s: the Charleston and joy-riding in light aircraft.

Above A café beside the Thames, 1926, and dancing to the strains of the Palm Court Orchestra.

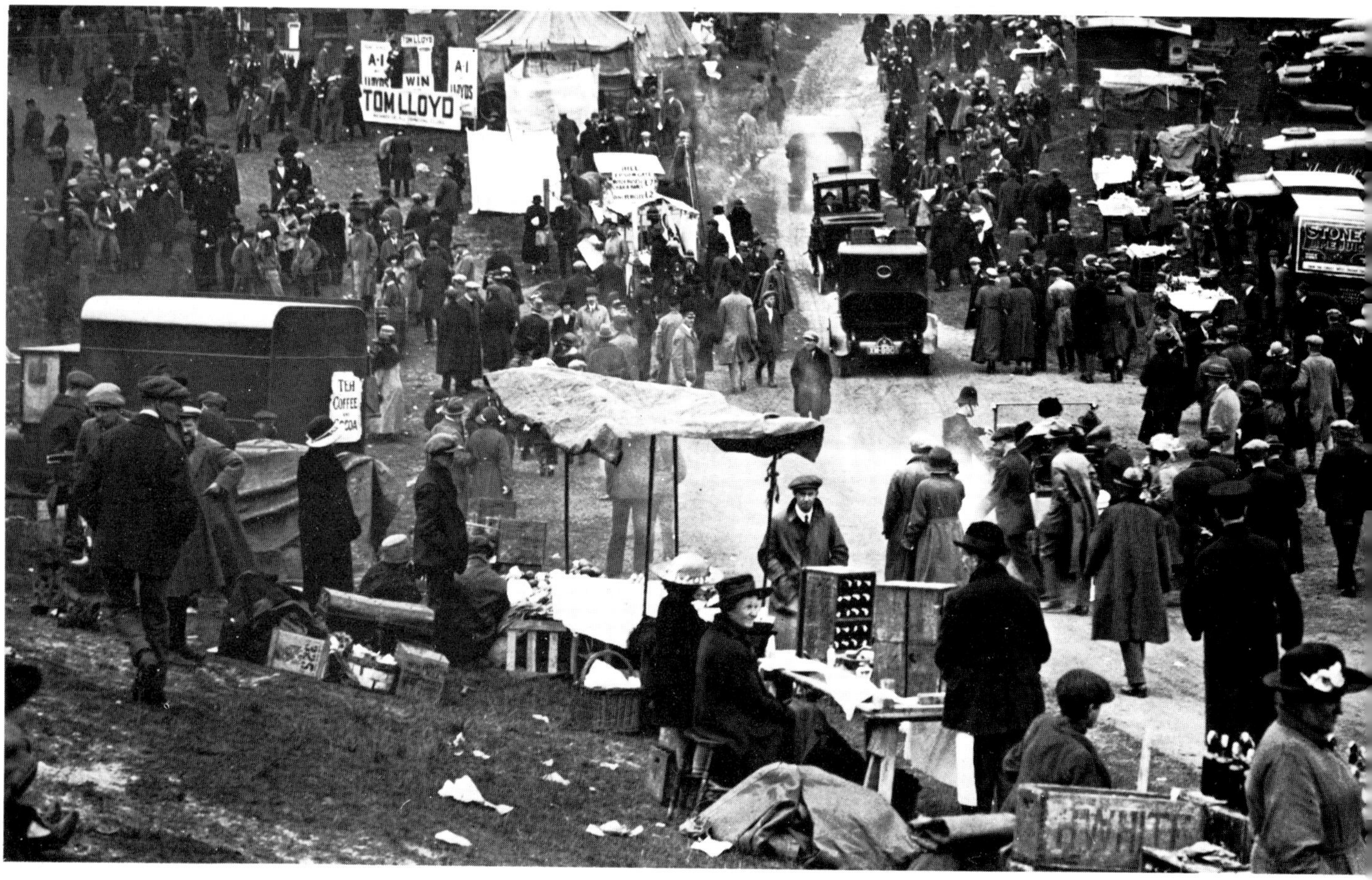
TOM LLOYD
WIN

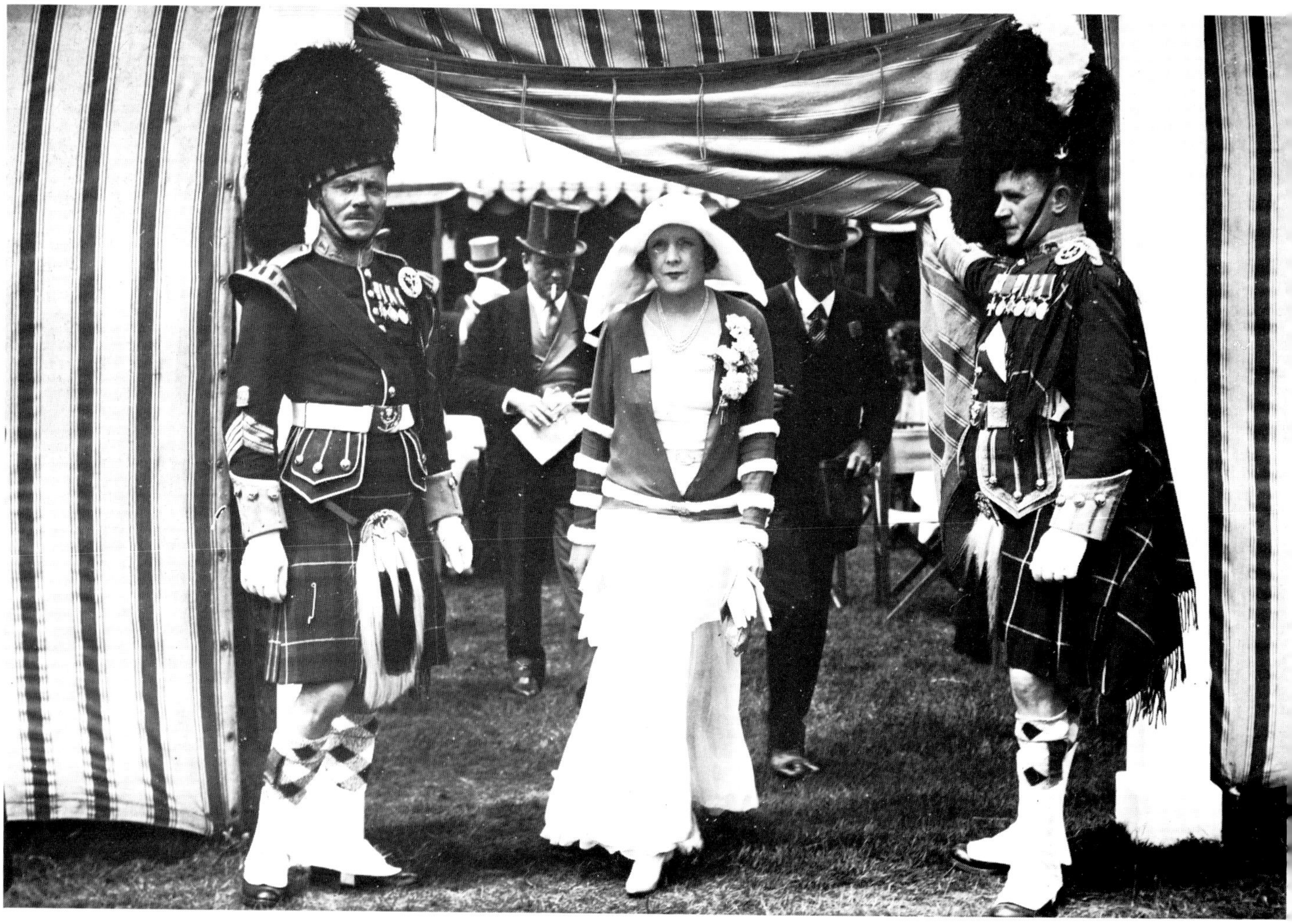

Top left Crowds flock to Epsom Downs for a view of the Derby in June 1923.

Left At Ascot in June 1930, the celebrated Miss McCorquodale leaves the Highland Brigade enclosure.

Above Paying for the pleasure of a London park, 1923.

August afternoon — cricket on the green at Banstead, Surrey, in 1936.

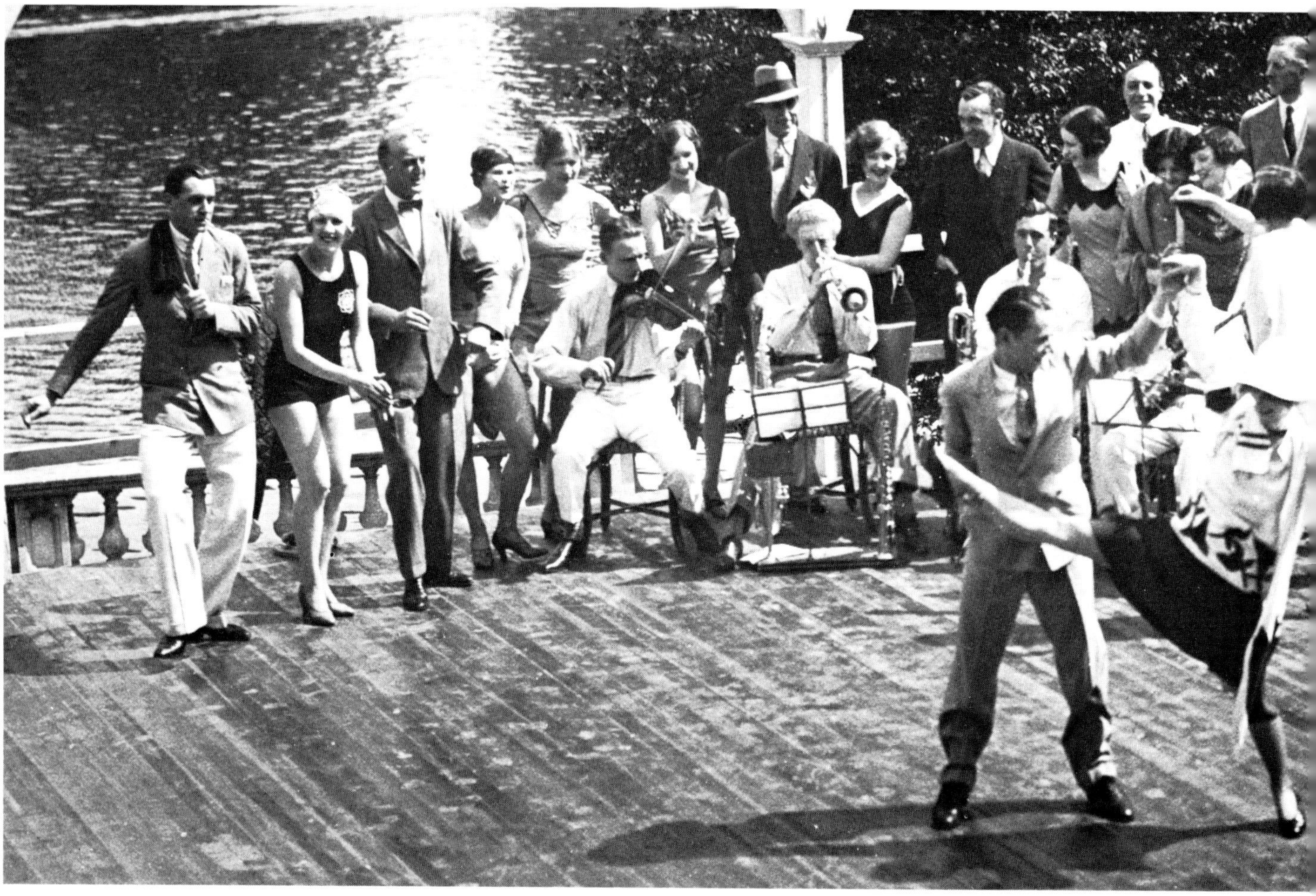

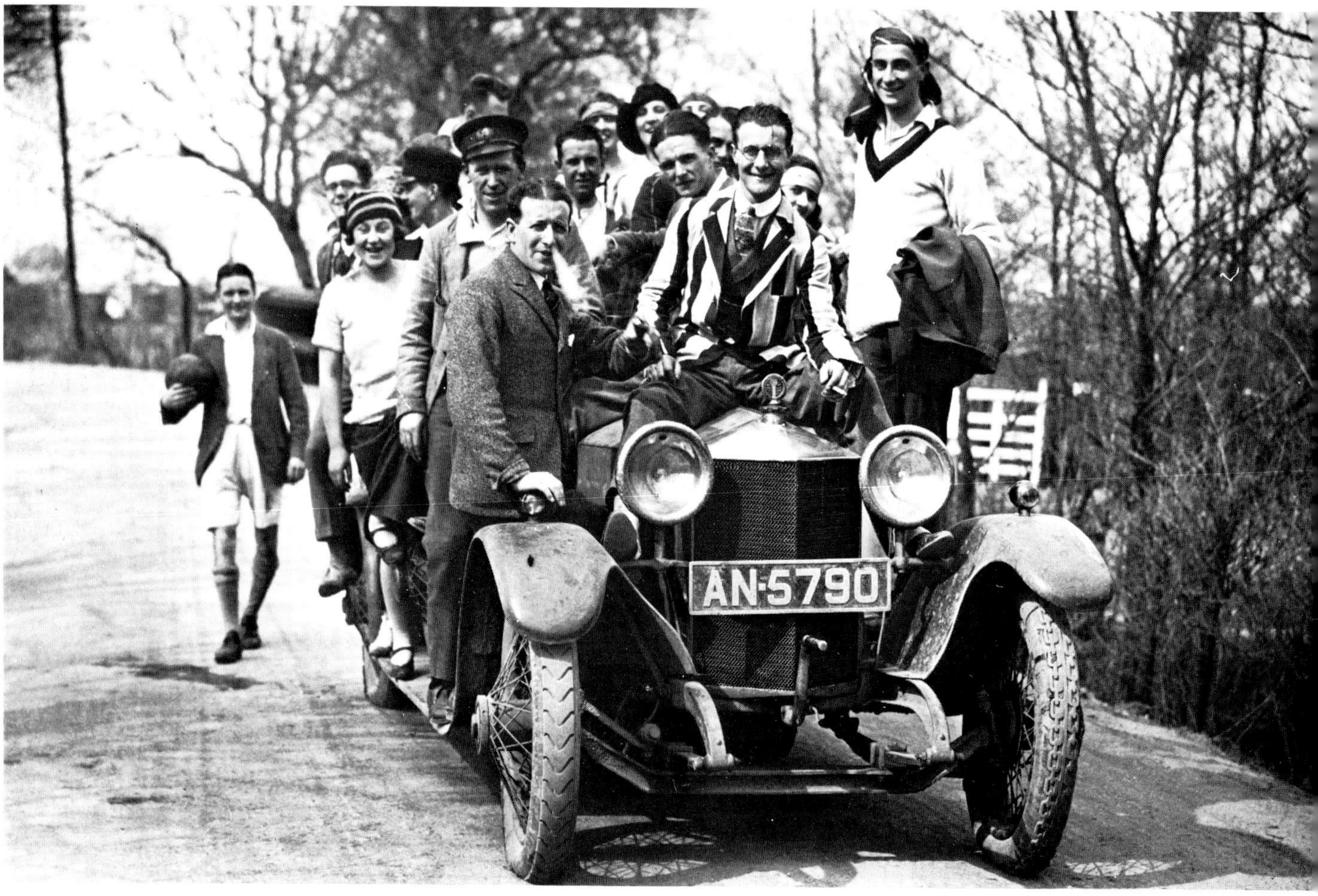
AN-5790

Left Jazz by the Thames, summer 1924.

Below left Off to the beach at Canvey Island in 1923.

Below Boating on the Thames near Richmond, June 1925.

Above A Glaswegian walks his dogs, 1939. Greyhound racing became an organised sport during the thirties.

Above right and right Quiet pastimes in the Elephant and Castle, South London, 1949.

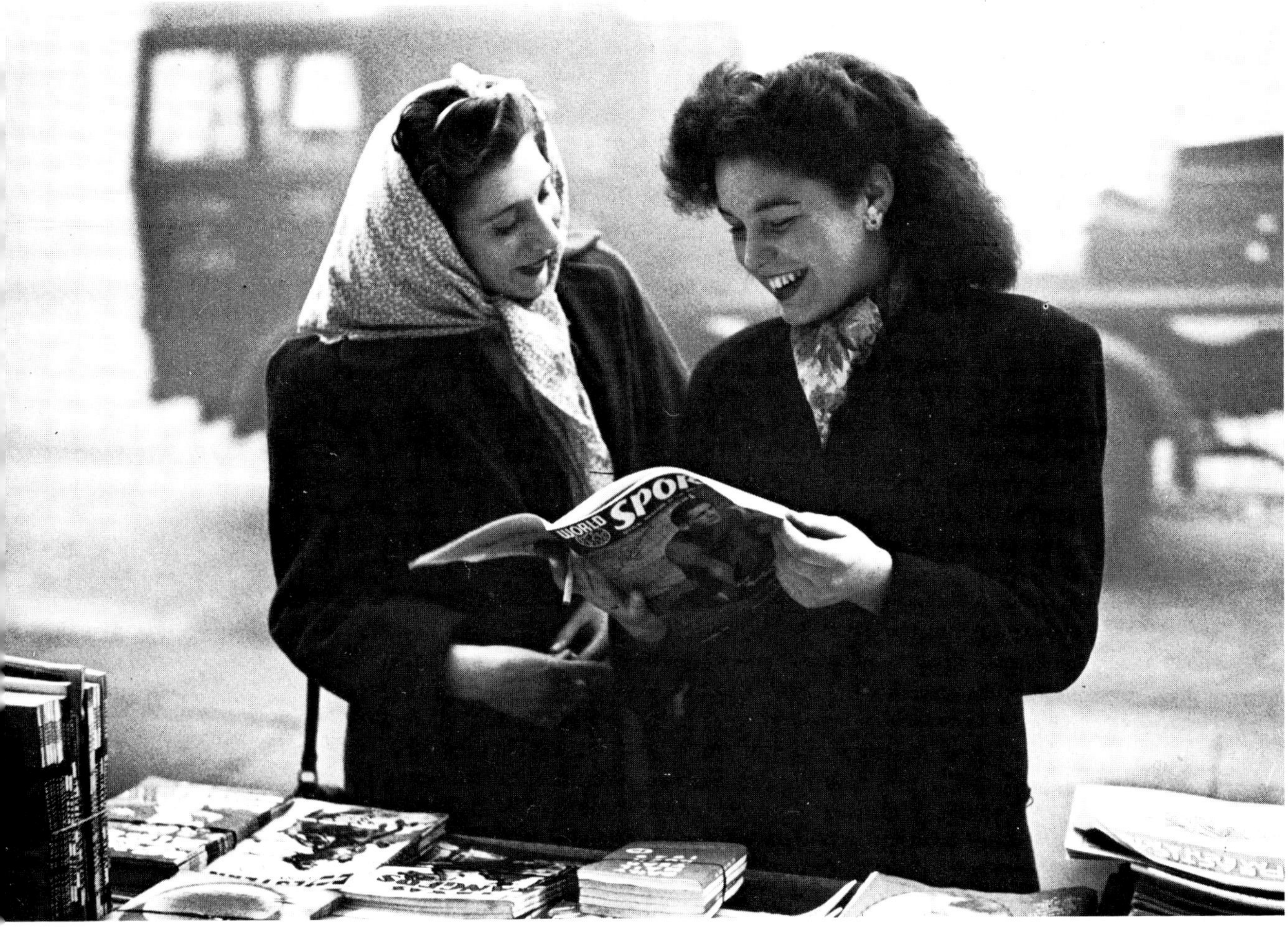
WORLD

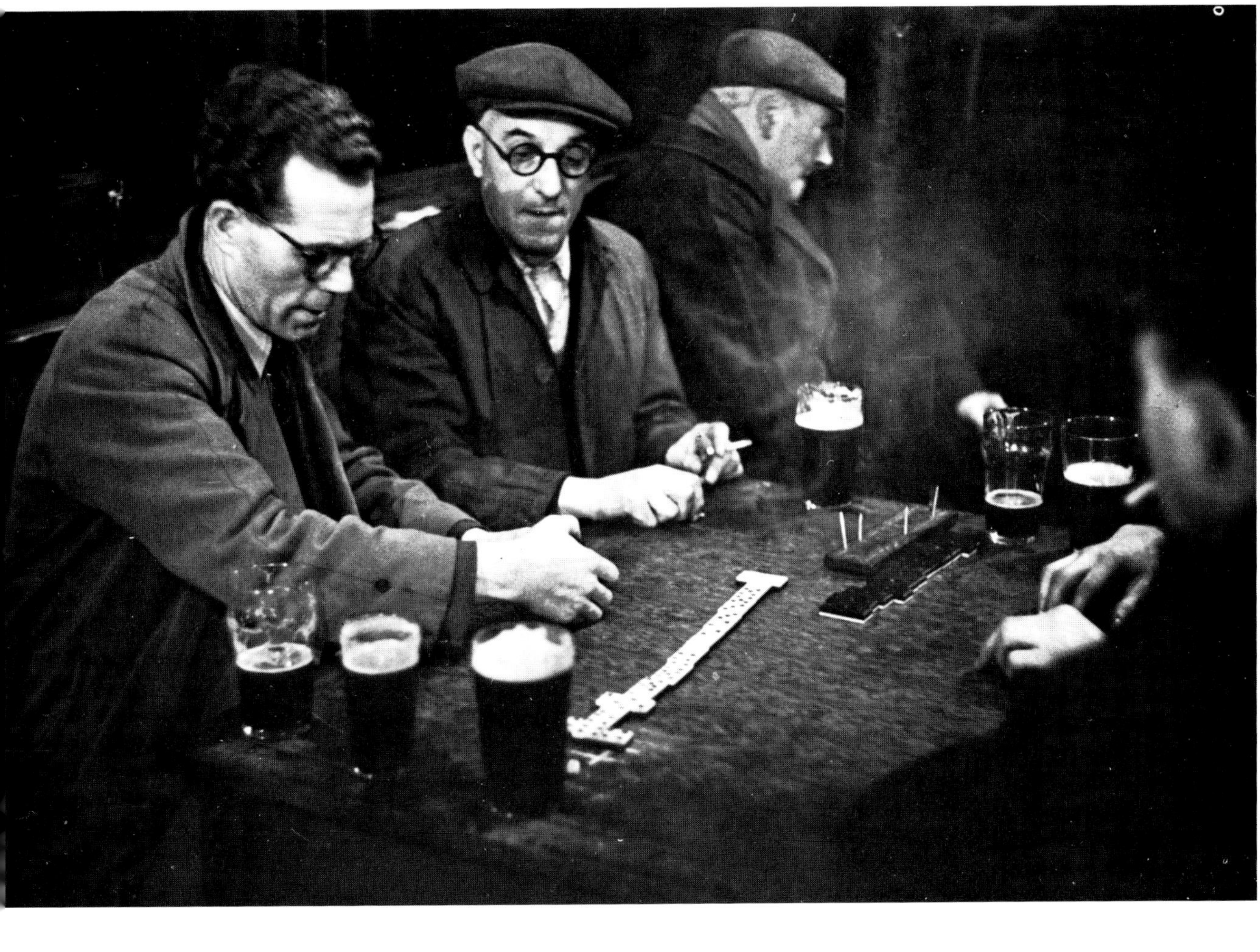

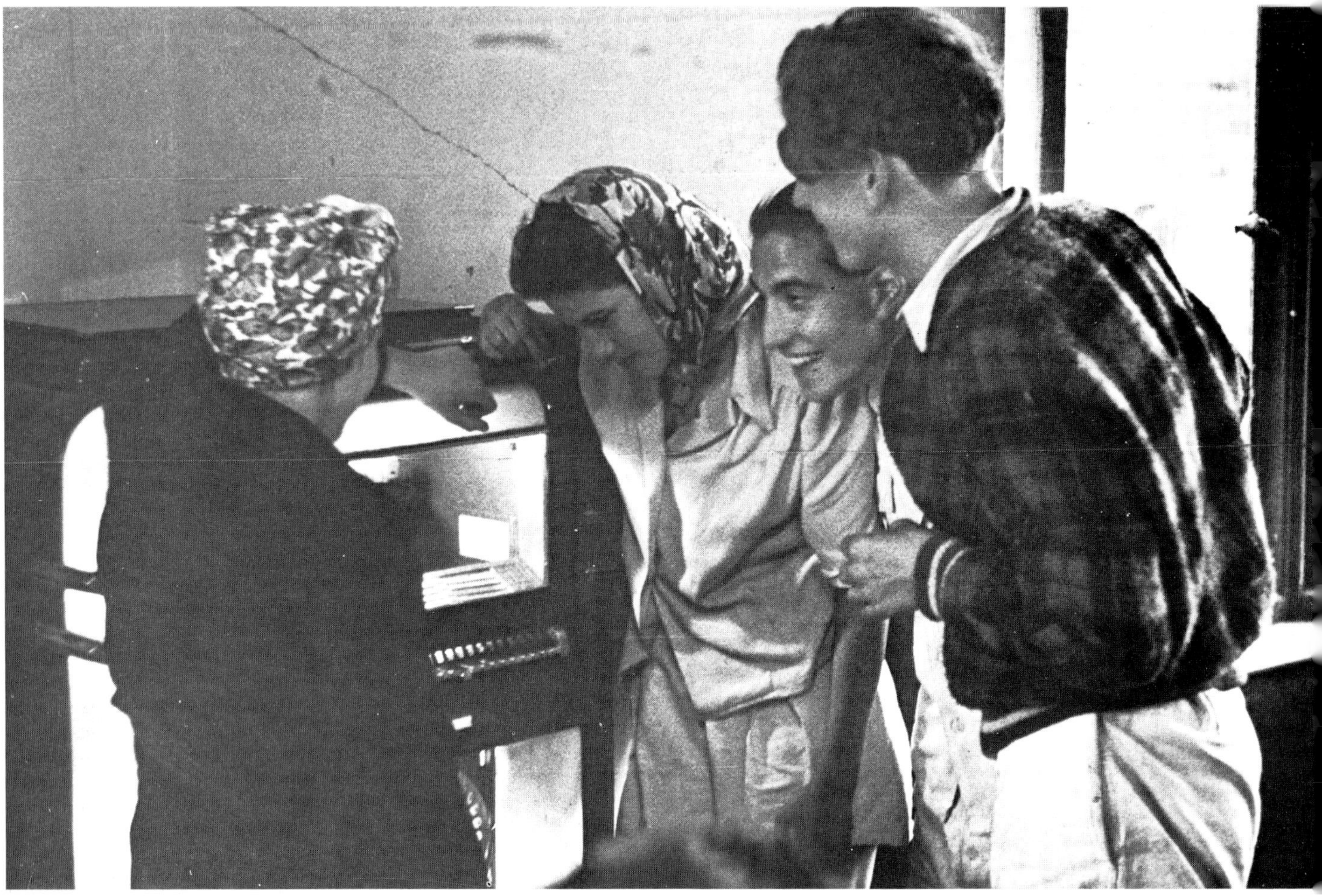

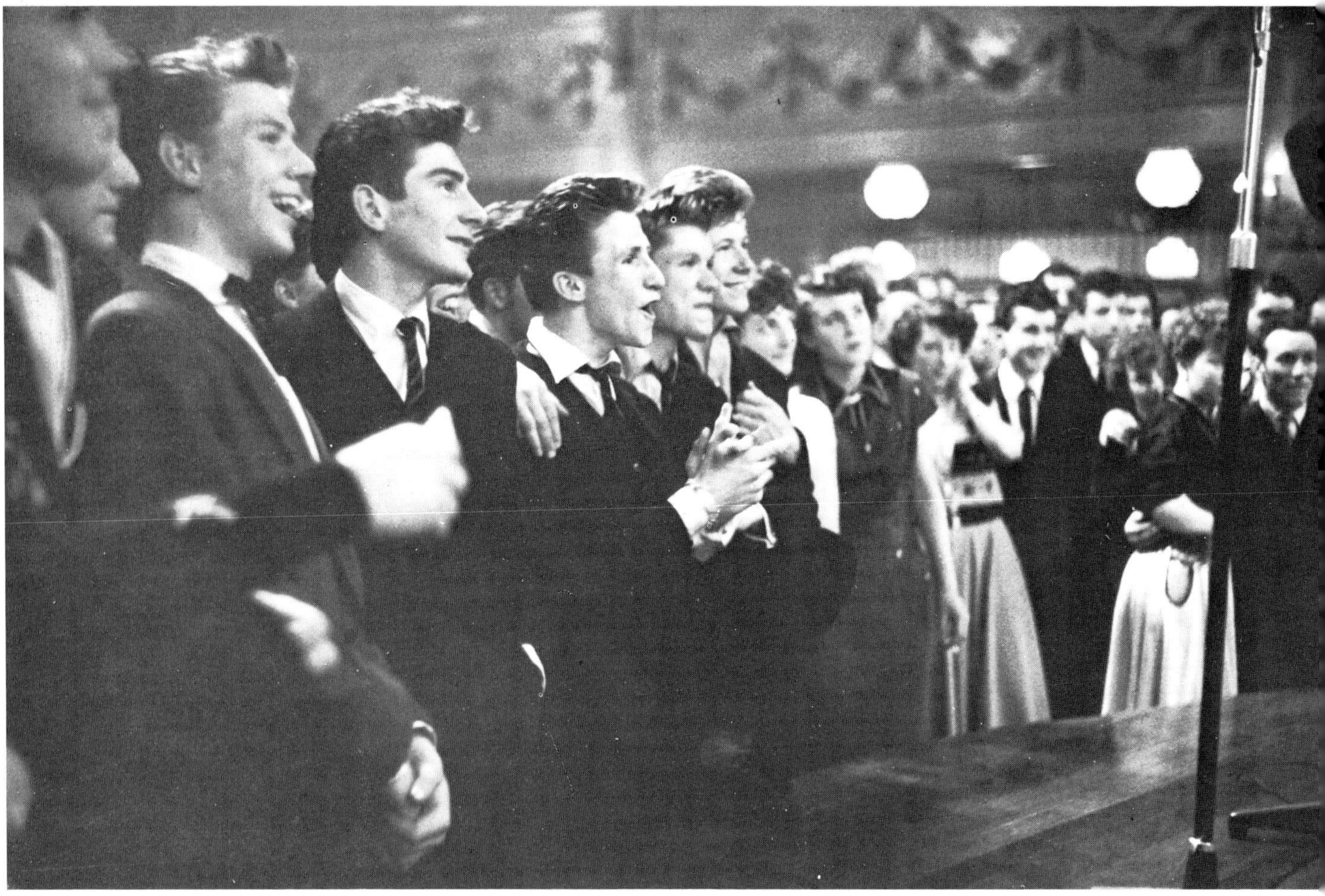

Top left The 'juke-box' arrives, 1949.

Above Ballroom dancing, courtesy of Victor Sylvester's band, in 1954.

Left 'Teddy boys' at the Mecca Dance Hall in Tottenham, 1954.

Mass-produced fun at Billy Butlin's holiday camp at Skegness, 1939. By the
1950s holiday camps were big business.

The traditional family holiday — ice cream and sandals on Margate beach, 1955.

Home and Family

Above Classical lines of a Victorian mansion, Somerges Court, at Westerham in Kent, 1864.

Right The cluttered drawing room of an academic at Downing College, Cambridge, in the 1870s.

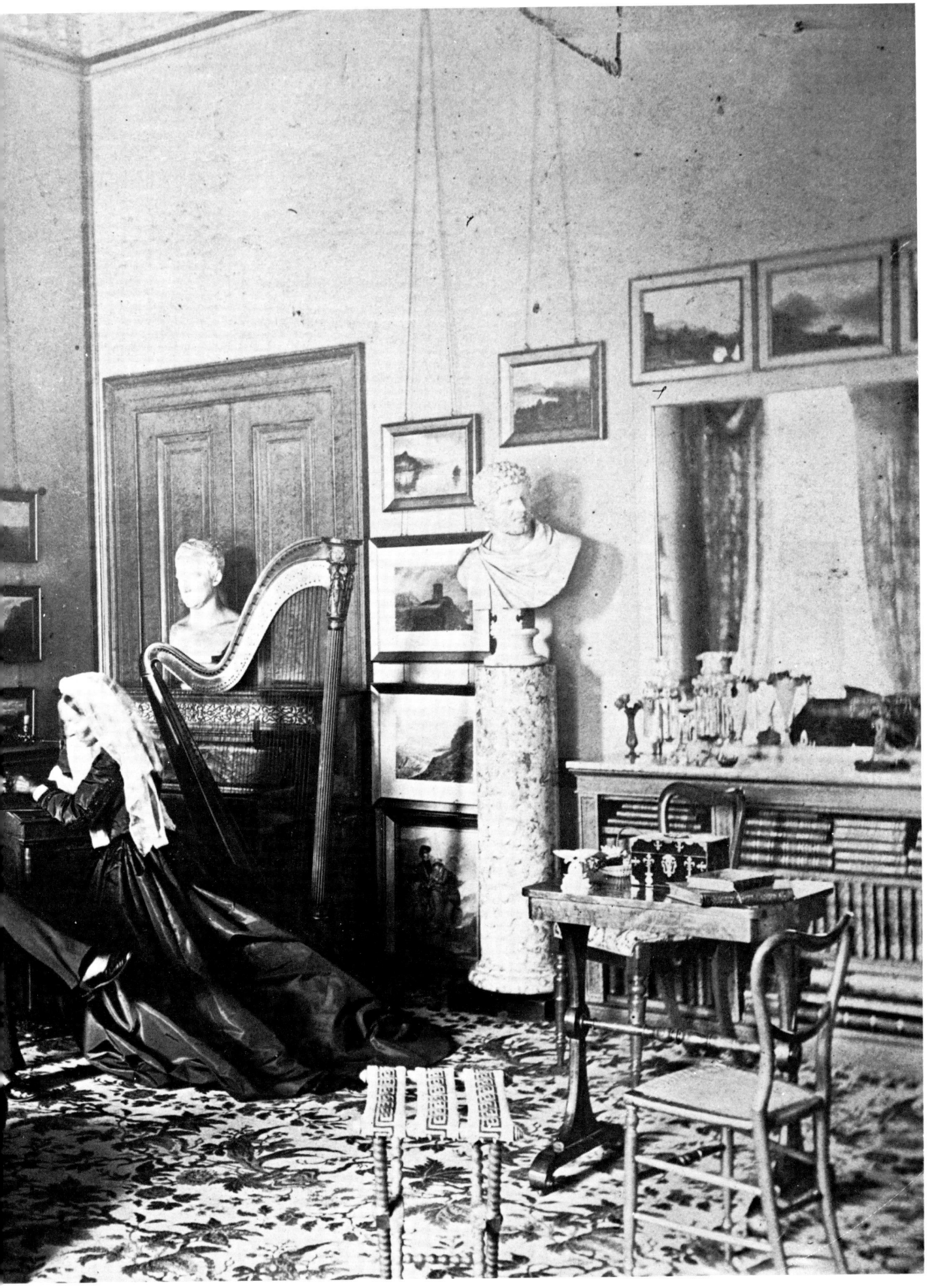

The home of a crofter in the Shetland Islands, *c*.1900.

Far left Servants cleaning fish, 1855.

Above Tenement dwellers share water taps and a central gutter.

Left A gypsy caravan in London, 1874.

Above A country family, 1859.

Right The sporting family, 1864.

Above Afternoon tea with the family, *c.*1890.

Above right Two families united at a wedding party in 1865.

Right Three generations in an Edwardian sitting room.

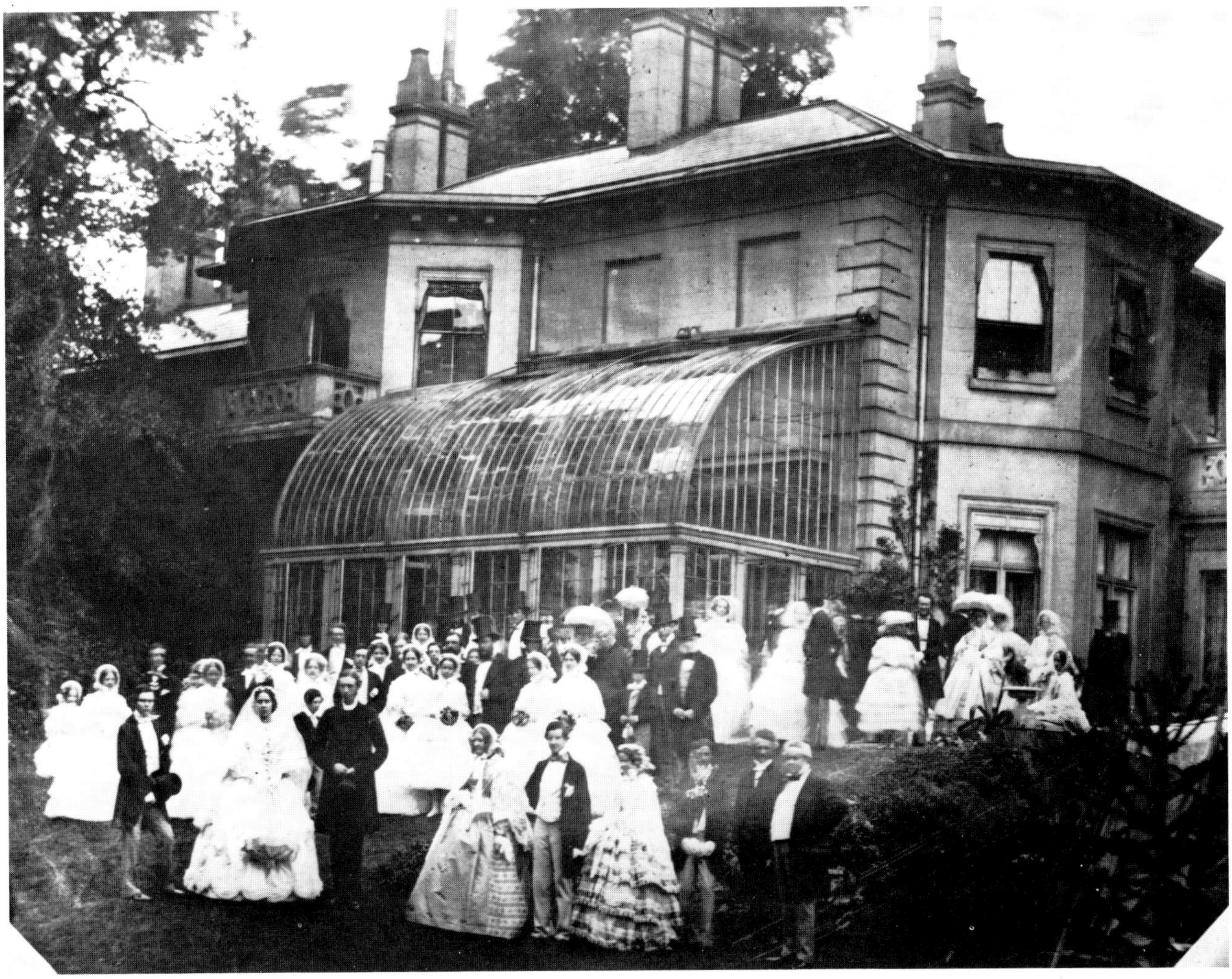

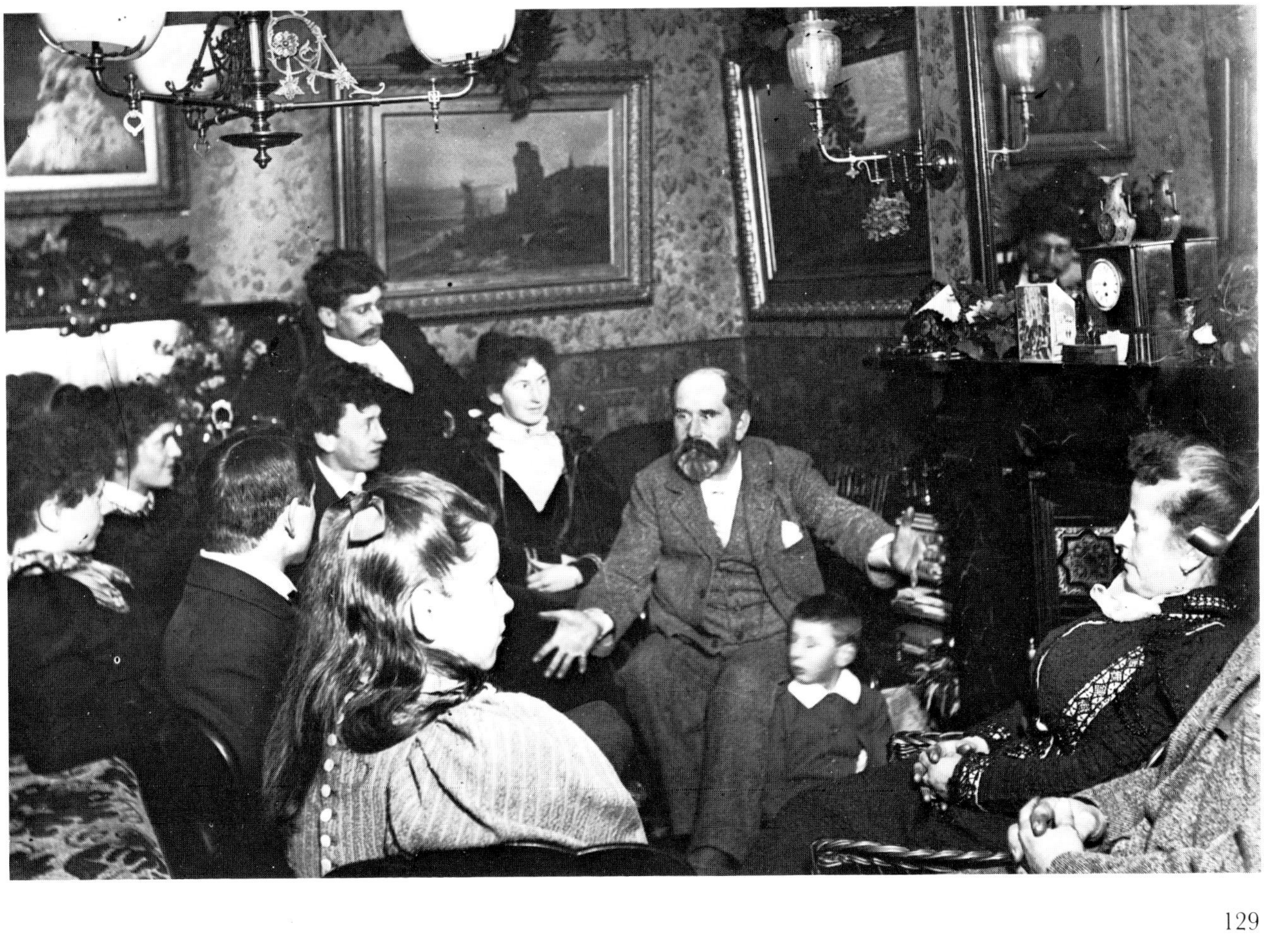

Remnants of an older world after the First World War.

Above Debutantes at a coming-out party.

Above right Relaxing on the tennis court, 1923.

Right The maid prepares tea, 1927.

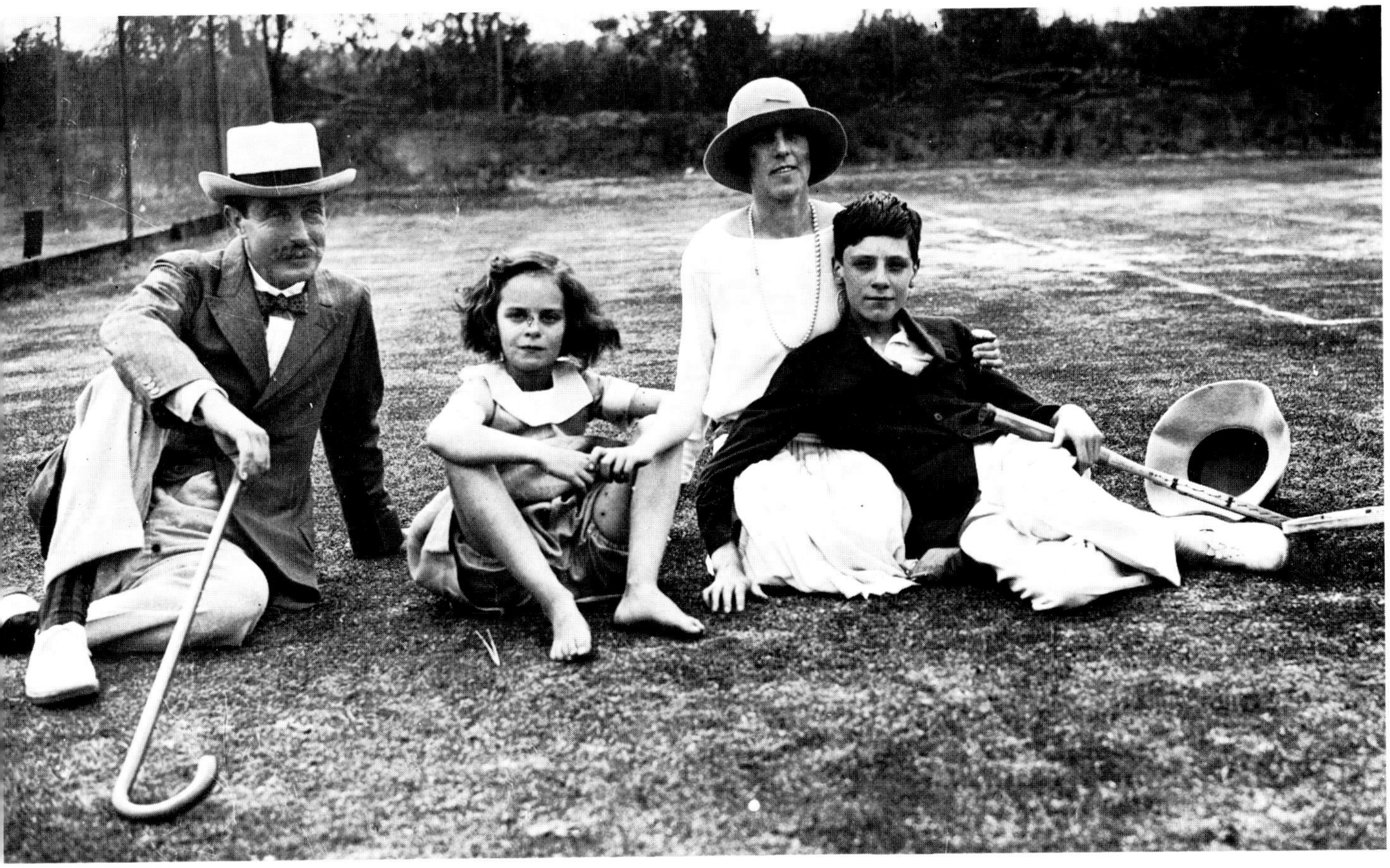

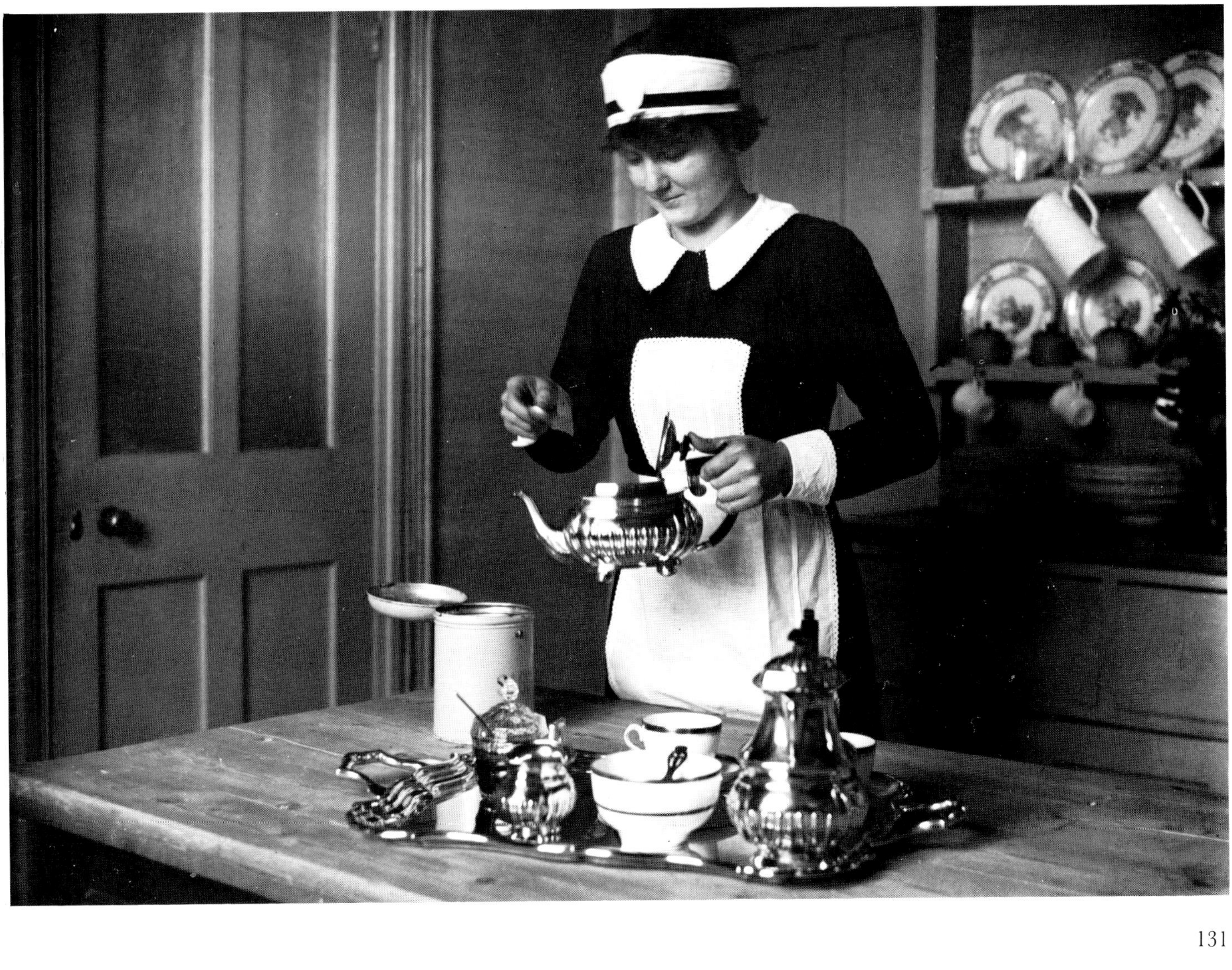

Far left Despondency on the streets of Wigan in 1939.

Above At home in the Welsh valleys.

Left A bath for a Durham miner, 1934.

Children at play in London's East End, 1933.

Early morning in Liverpool, 1954.

Above left Nursemaids wait to see the bride at a wedding at St Paul's in Knightsbridge, 1938.

Above The end of a good day's shooting, 1954.

Left Visiting the hounds of the Craven Hunt at Baydon Manor near Swindon in October, 1931.

A daily chore for a large family in Yorkshire, in 1940, with 13 of the 17 children still at home

An evacuee family from London settle in with a miner's family in the Midlands in 1945

Above Back-to-back houses in an old industrial estate in Birmingham, 1954.
Neighbours were never far away.

Above right The one-room flat for a family of four in Brixton, London, 1954.

Right Suburban Dagenham in 1956.

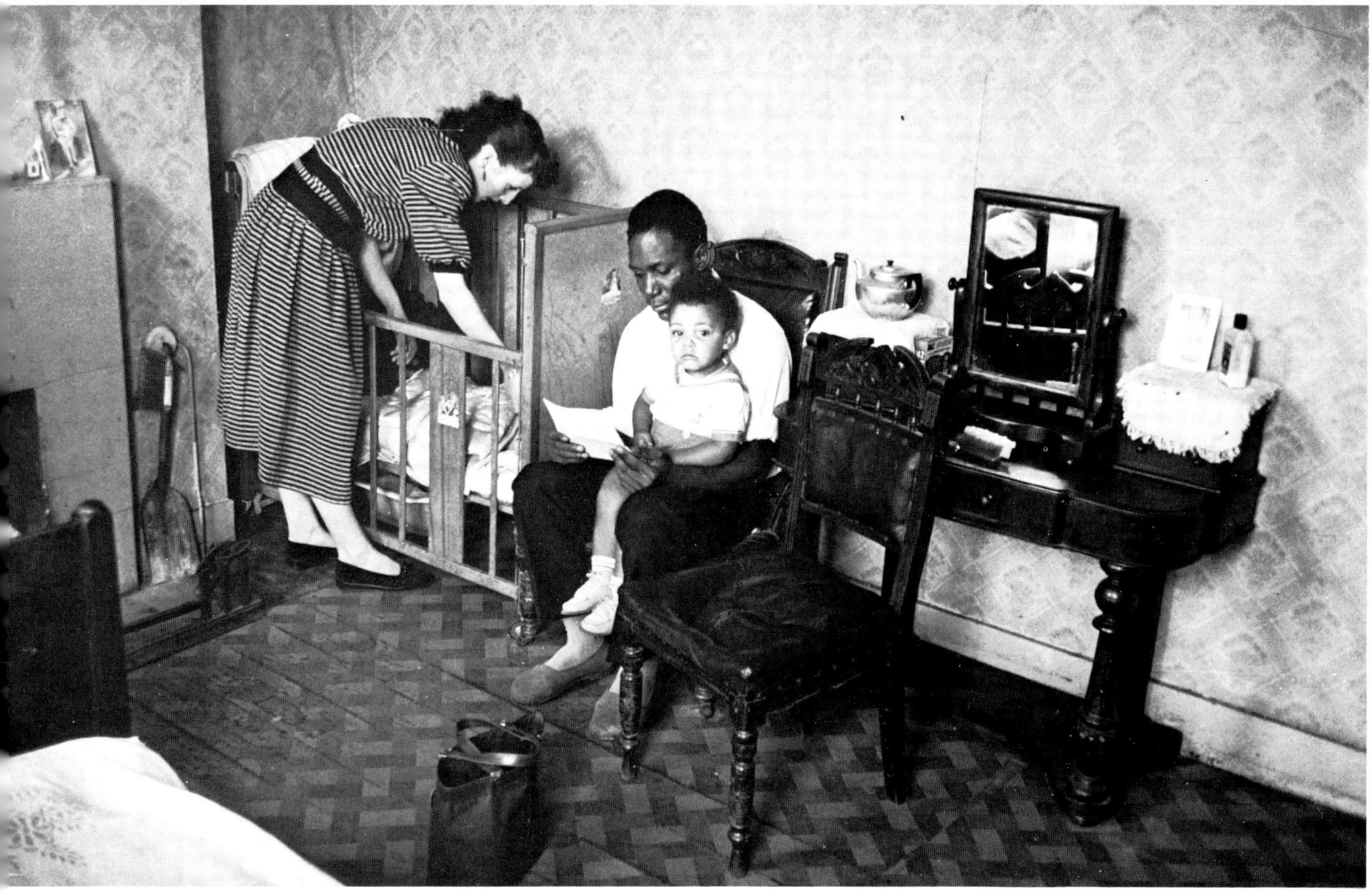

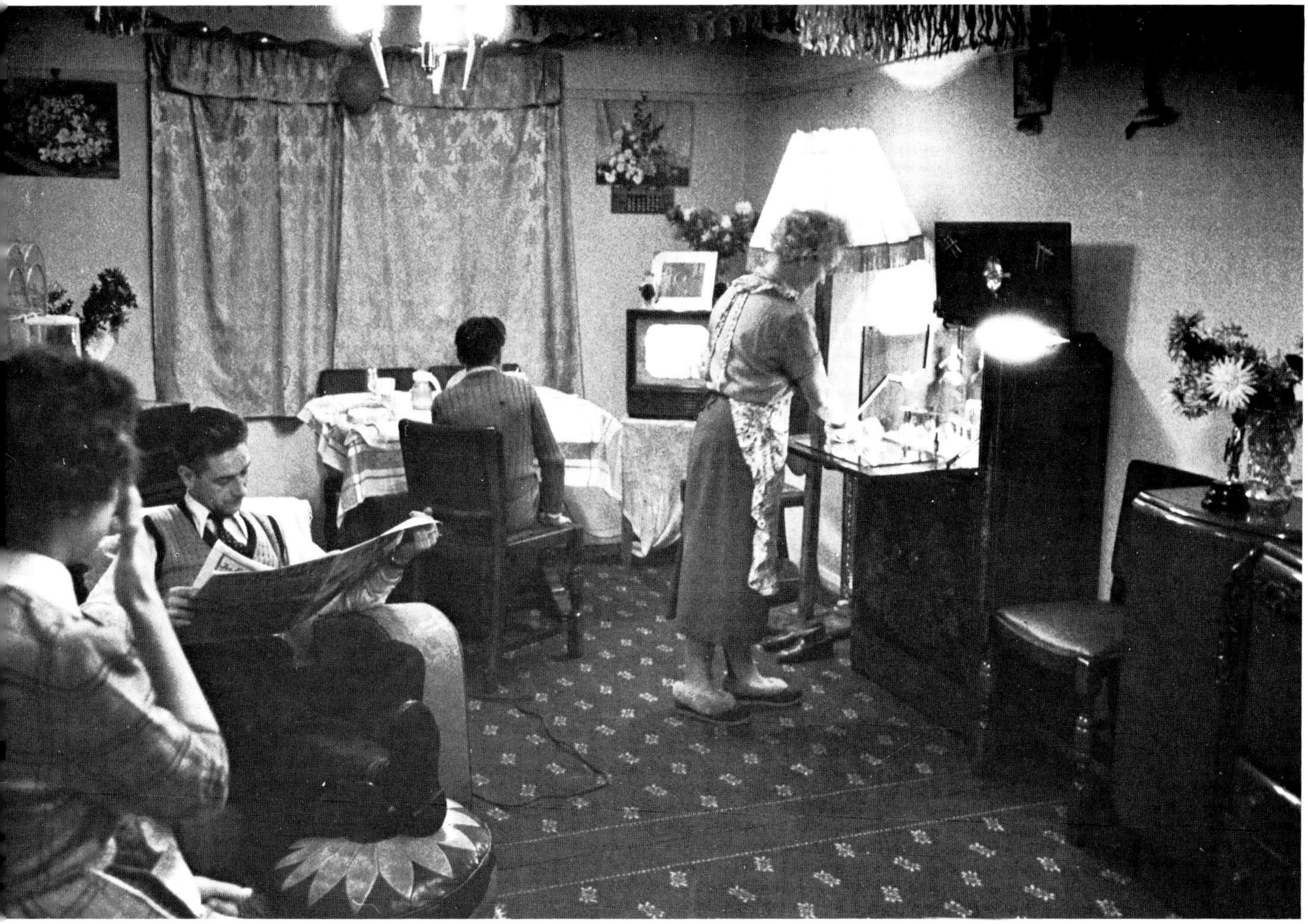

Miles apart in 1955: the tiny balcony of a modern flat
and the cosy hearth of a country cottage

Politics

Above Benjamin Disraeli, Earl of Beaconsfield, Prime Minister in 1868 and 1874-80, who restored the right of peaceful picketing to the unions.

Right The third anniversary of the '8 hours a day' movement in 1858. Skilled workers led the campaign for the shorter working day.

Above Karl Marx, who worked in London from 1858 until his death in 1883.

Above right Friedrich Engels, Marx's partner, who followed him to England from Germany.

Far right Beatrice and Sydney Webb, prominent among the Fabian theorists around the turn of the century.

148

Left The Match Girls who won their strike at Bryant and Mays factory in 1888.

Above left Annie Besant who led the Match Girls' strike. This photograph was taken 23 years before, when she was 18.

Above right Keir Hardie in 1892. He was to be the first Socialist in Parliament.

Above Charles Stewart Parnell, leader of the Irish Nationalist Home Rule Party in the late nineteenth century.

Right William Ewart Gladstone, many times Liberal Prime Minister between the 1860s and 1890s. His commitment to Irish Home Rule irretrievably damaged his party.

Simultaneous strikes by local unions threatened to paralyse whole industries in the years before the First World War.

Above Ben Tillet, who formed the National Transport Workers Federation, addressing strikers in 1911.

Right A police escort for imported meat during the 1912 Dock strike.

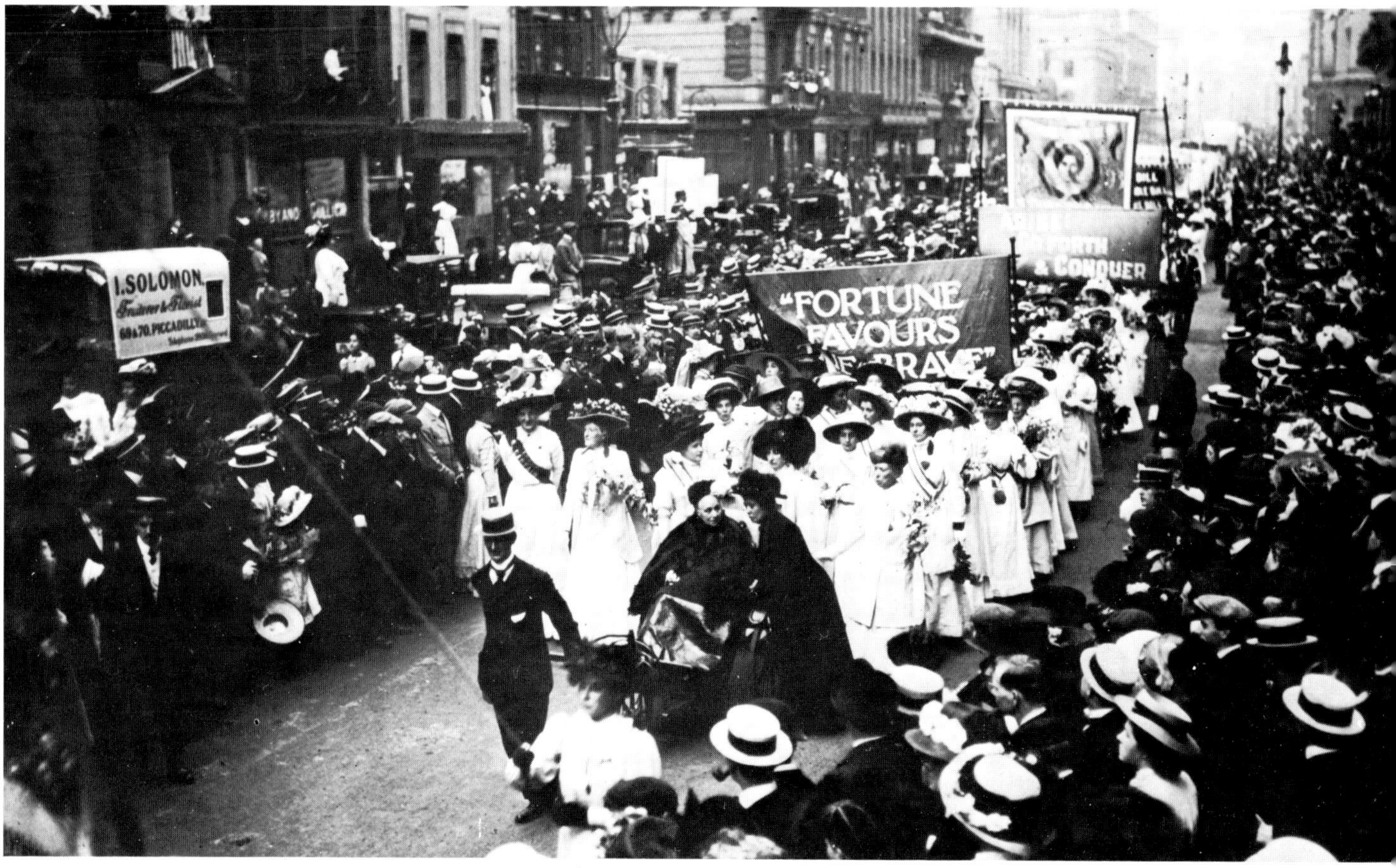
I. SOLOMON
68 & 70 PICCADILLY
“FORTUNE
FAVOURS
& CONQUER

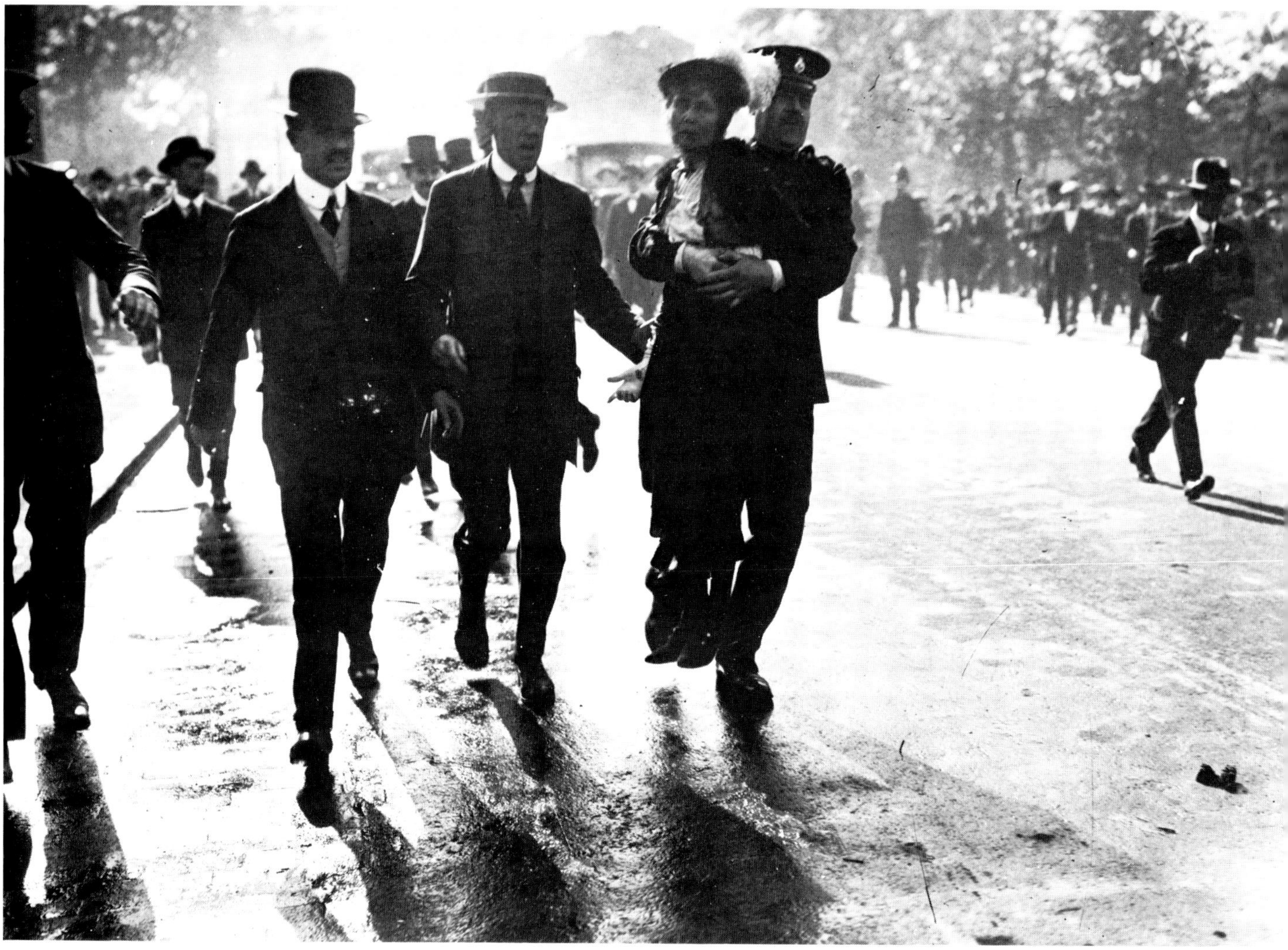

Above left A demonstration by the Women's Social and Political Union in 1911. Demands for women's suffrage were consistently refused until 1918.

Left Mrs Emmeline Pankhurst, leader of the suffragettes, arrested outside Buckingham Palace in July, 1914.

Above Lloyd George, the Chancellor, and Home Secretary Winston Churchill, members of the Liberal government in 1915.

Above Tom Mann, veteran labour leader and communist, outside Bow Street Magistrates Court in October 1925.

Above right During the General Strike in 1926 — police protection for volunteer bus drivers.

Right The third day of the Strike, June 1926 — strikers watch a disabled bus being towed away in Southwark, London.

ALDWYCH
1
SALOON BAR
B 4913

MAURICE MOSCOVITCH
"THE GREAT LOVER"
SHAFTESBURY
HARTLEY'S
Thomas Tilling Limited
12

The depression of the thirties brought a further polarization in politics: the National Union of Unemployed Workers organized hunger marches, and Sir Oswald Mosley assumed leadership of the British Union of Fascists.

Above left and left During the three-hundred mile march from Jarrow to Westminster in 1936, unemployed workers pass through Bedfordshire.

Above Sir Oswald Mosley saluting a fascist rally in southeast London, October 1937.

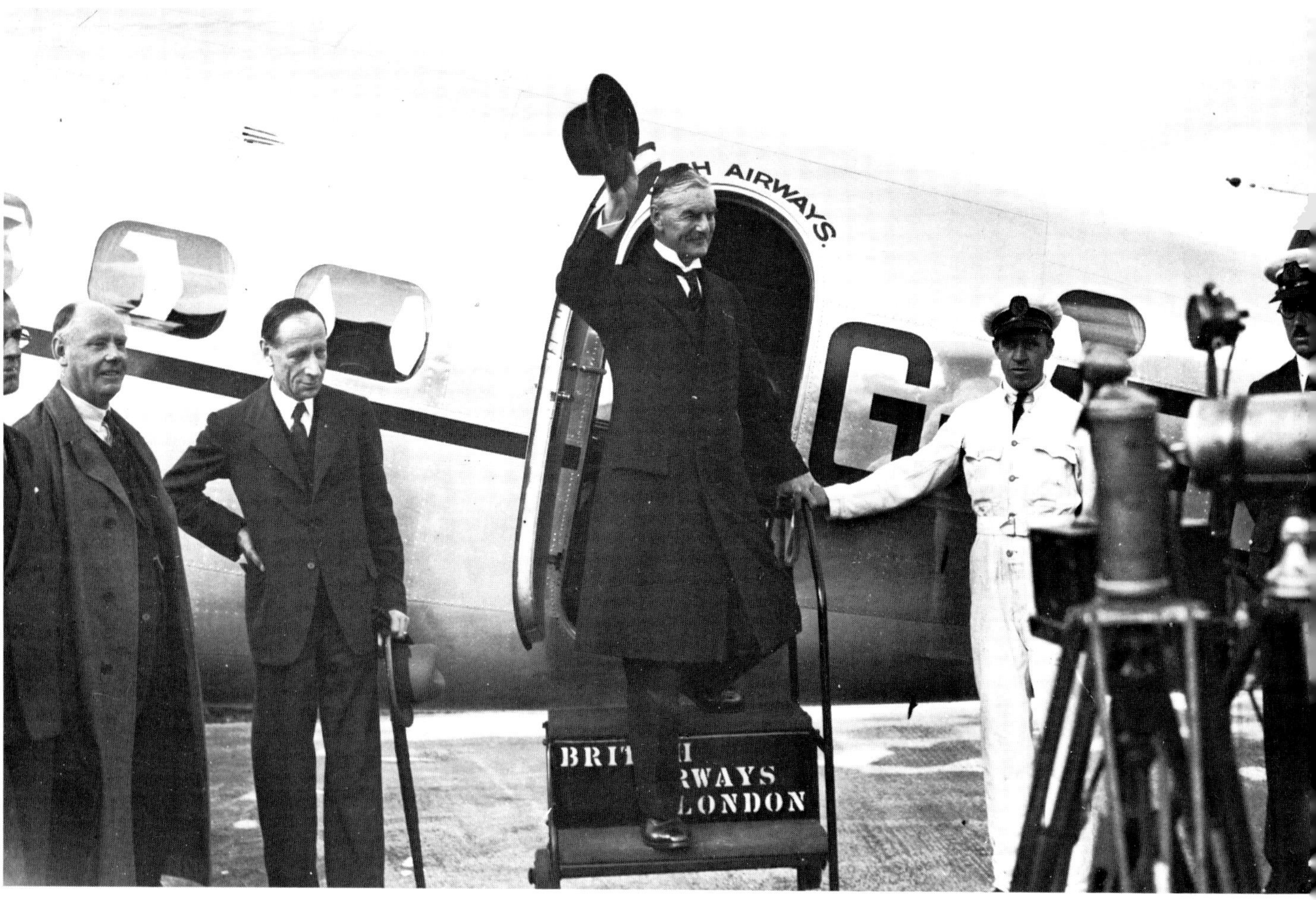
AIRWAYS.
LONDON

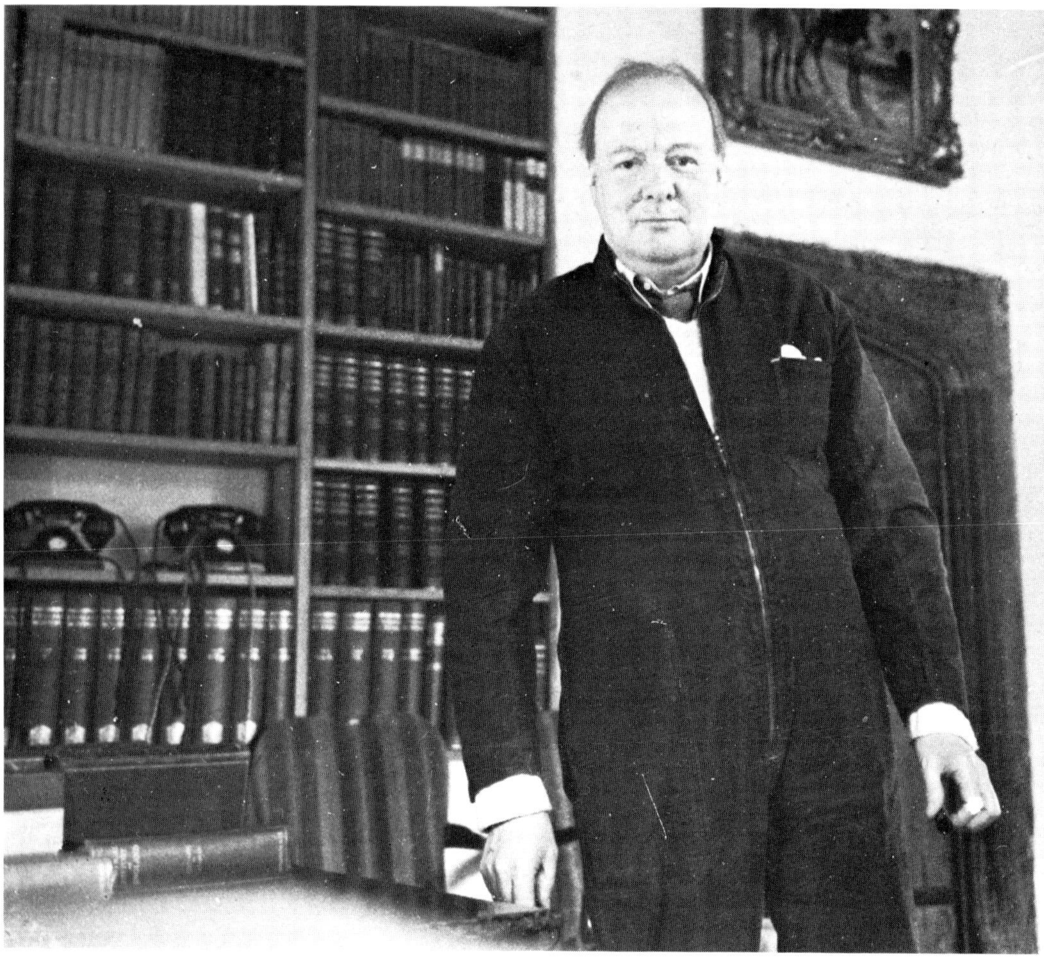

Above left Prime Minister Neville Chamberlain flies to Munich in September 1938 to meet Hitler for the second time.

Left Winston Churchill at Chartwell in 1939, wearing his favourite siren suit. The following year he replaced Chamberlain as Prime Minister, heading a coalition government.

Above Sir William Beveridge at a Liberal meeting in London in 1943. The Beveridge Report, which would form the basis of the Welfare State legislation, had been published in 1942.

Left Clement Attlee campaigning in Walthamstow, London, in 1950. The following year his Labour Government was replaced by the Conservatives.

Above The Conservative Prime Minister, Sir Anthony Eden, arrives at the Guildhall in the City of London for a banquet in 1956. The Suez Crisis of the same year hastened Eden's retirement.

Wartime

Victoria's wars were fought in distant lands — the Crimea, Afghanistan, Egypt, South Africa. The Navy ruled the waves; the Army policed the Empire.

Above Boys training as 'powder monkeys' for the fleet in 1858.

Below Recruitment sergeants for the army at Westminster in 1877.

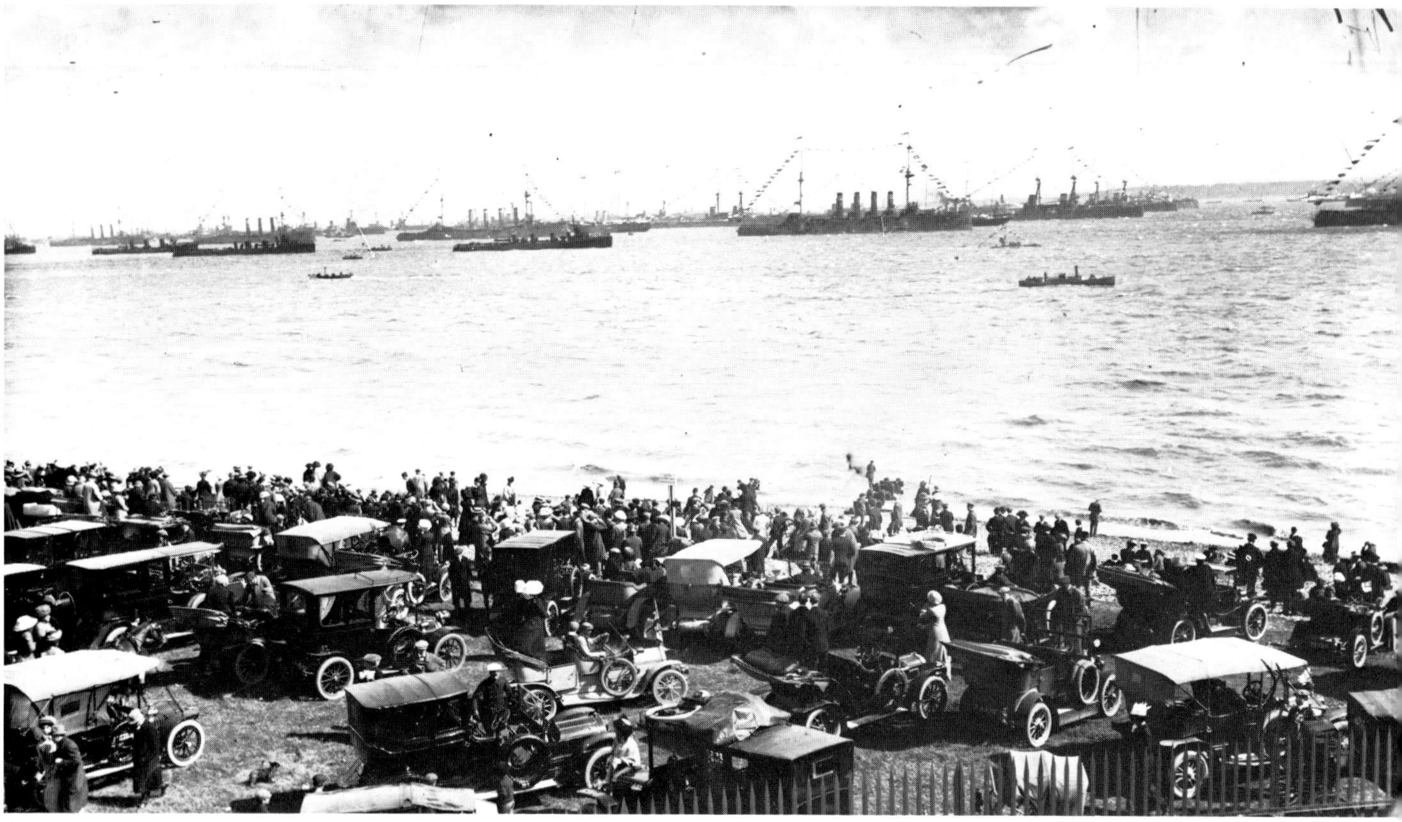

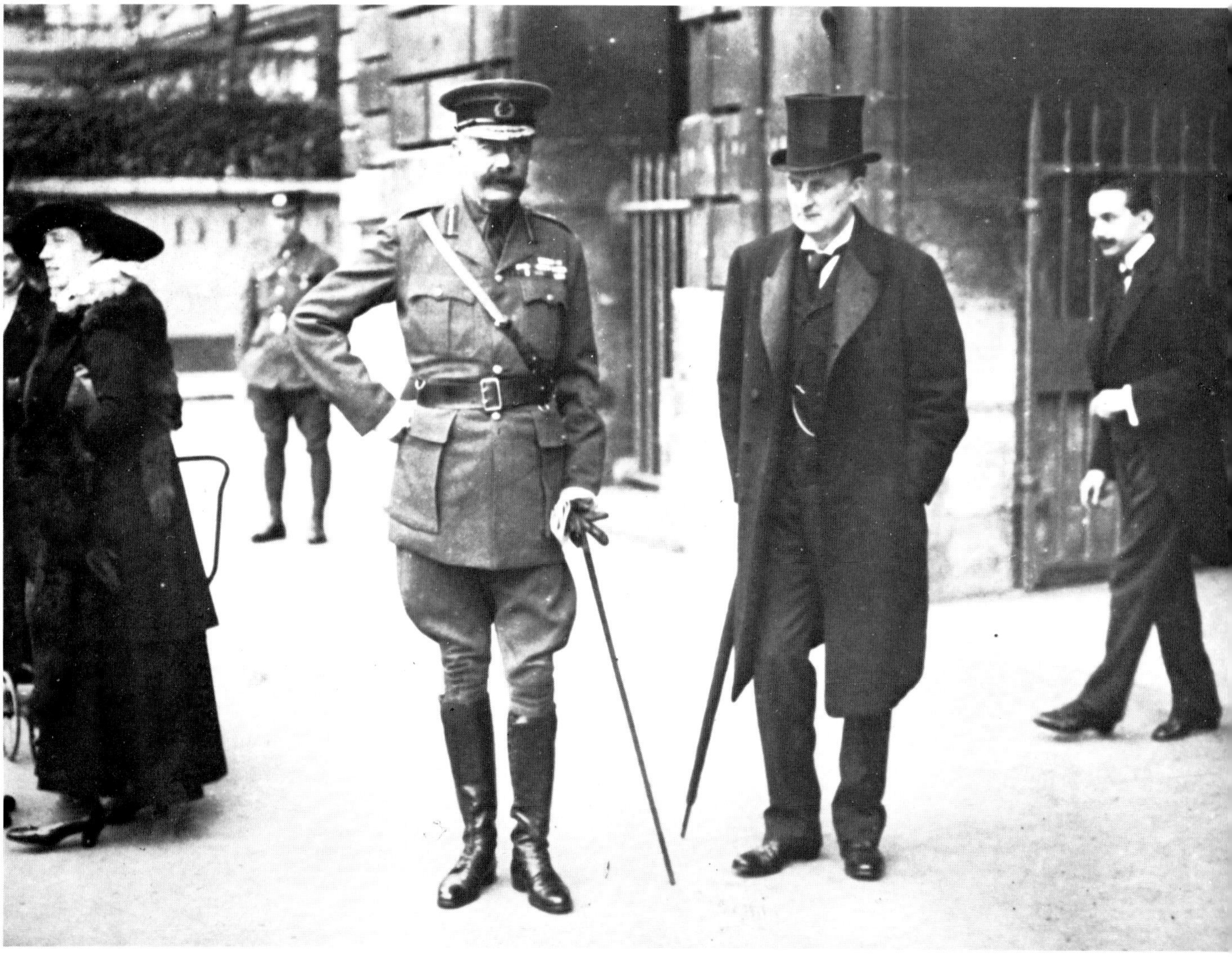

Britain entered the First World War with reckless enthusiasm. More than three million men had already volunteered when conscription began in 1916.

Above left A large crowd of motorists watch the fleet at the Spithead naval review in 1911.

Above Recruitment march for the King's Royal Rifle Corps in 1915.

Left Lord Kitchener, Minister of War, and the Foreign Secretary, Sir Edward Grey, in Paris the year before the War began.

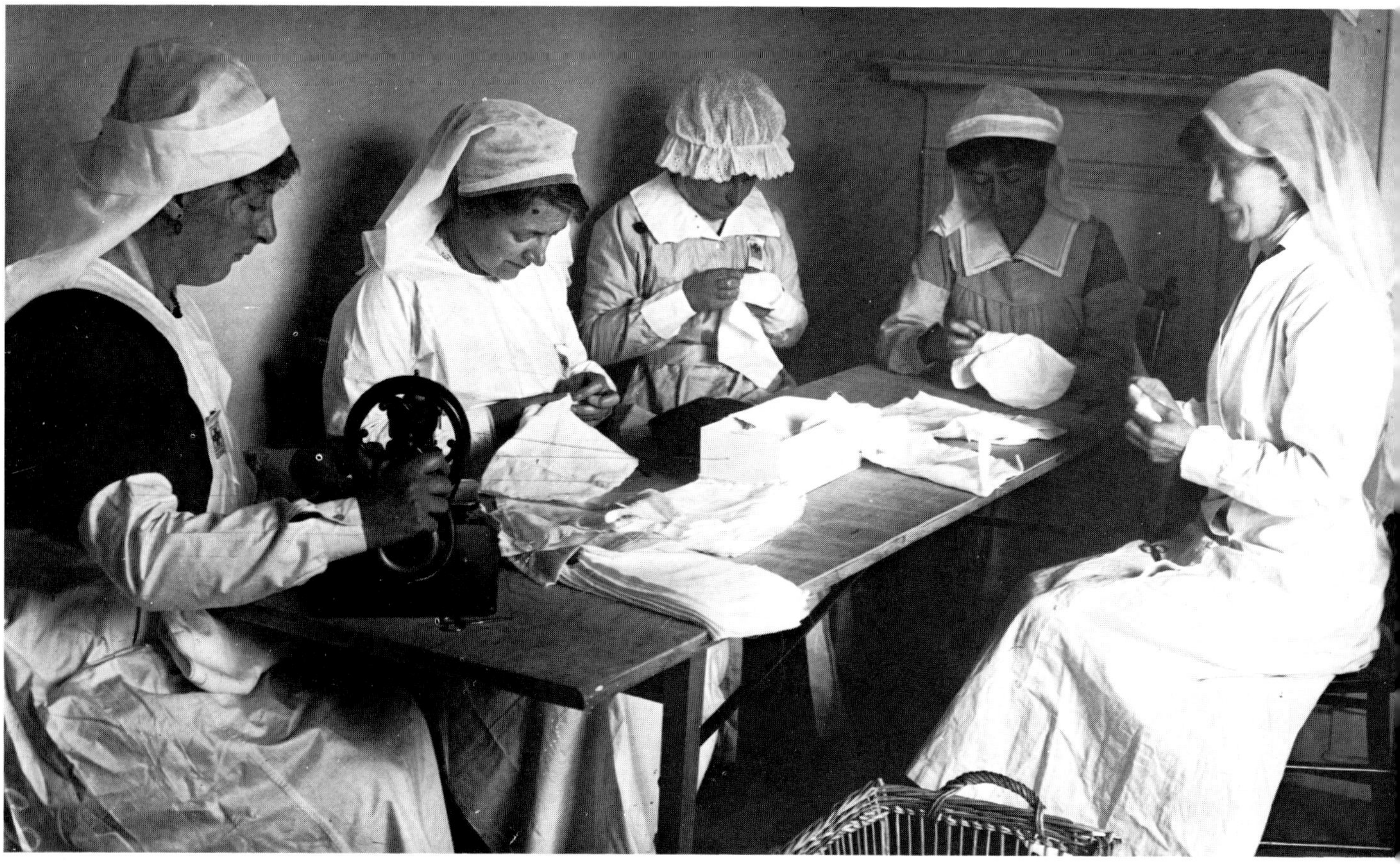

SOUTHAMPTON
ARMY STORES
LICHFIELD
SOUTHAMPTON
ARMY STORES
B.E.F
THE COMMISSIONER
BRITISH RED + SOCIETY
SALONICA FORCE
BOOKS
AUG. 26
THE COMMISSIONER
BRITISH RED + SOCIETY
SALONICA FORCE

Between 1914 and 1918 almost a million Britons were killed and more than twice that number wounded.

Above left Surgical dressings for the troops from a sewing circle.

Above Convalescent officers entertained by a violinist.

Left The British War Library, despatching books for the wounded to hospitals in France.

During the First World War, women did many jobs formerly reserved for men, particularly on farms, in offices and in engineering works. Some 400,000 left domestic service during the war.

Above New faces at the Mayfair Window Cleaning Co.

Right 'Feed the Guns' campaigning, to maintain munitions production in 1918.

Above An enduring novelty — the bus conductorette, 1917.

Right Celebrations on Armistice Day, 1918 — they went on for three days.

All over the country street parties
were held to celebrate the peace of
1918.

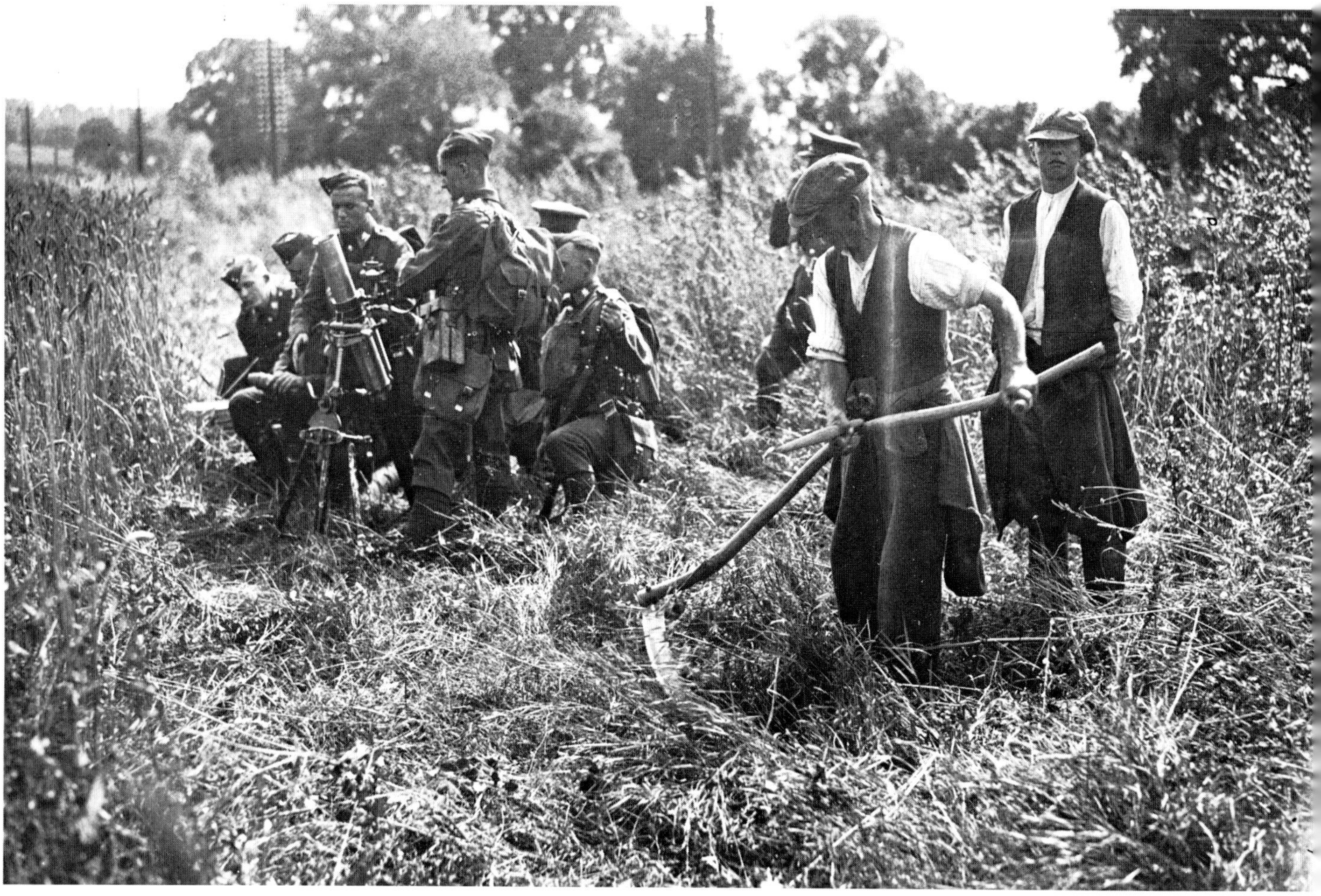

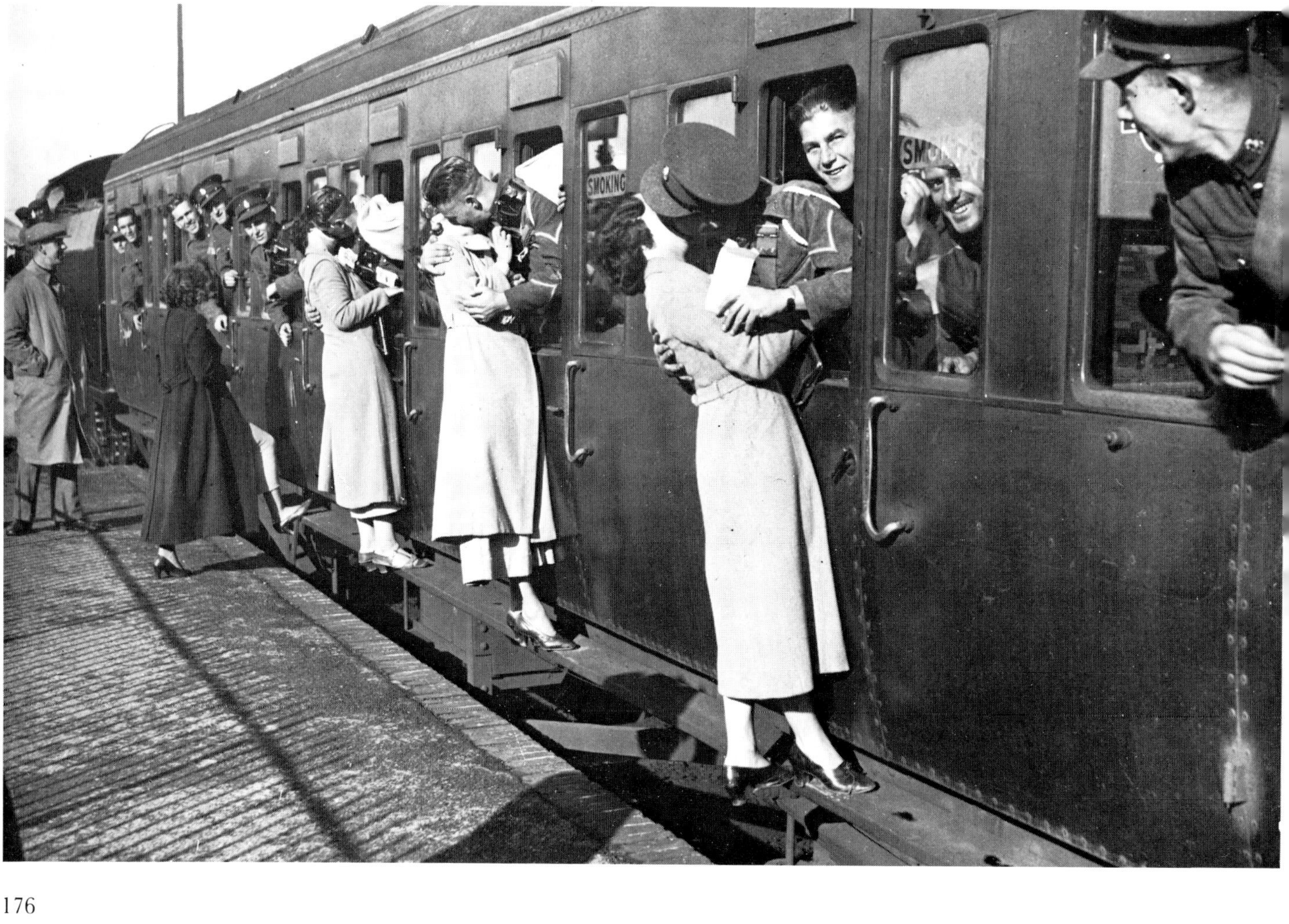
SMOKING

Above, far left Preparations for war, 1937 — Army manoeuvres in Hertfordshire with a trench mortar.

Far left The 7th Hussars embark for Egypt from Feltham in Middlesex in 1935.

Above Sunday, September 3rd, 1939. War with Germany.

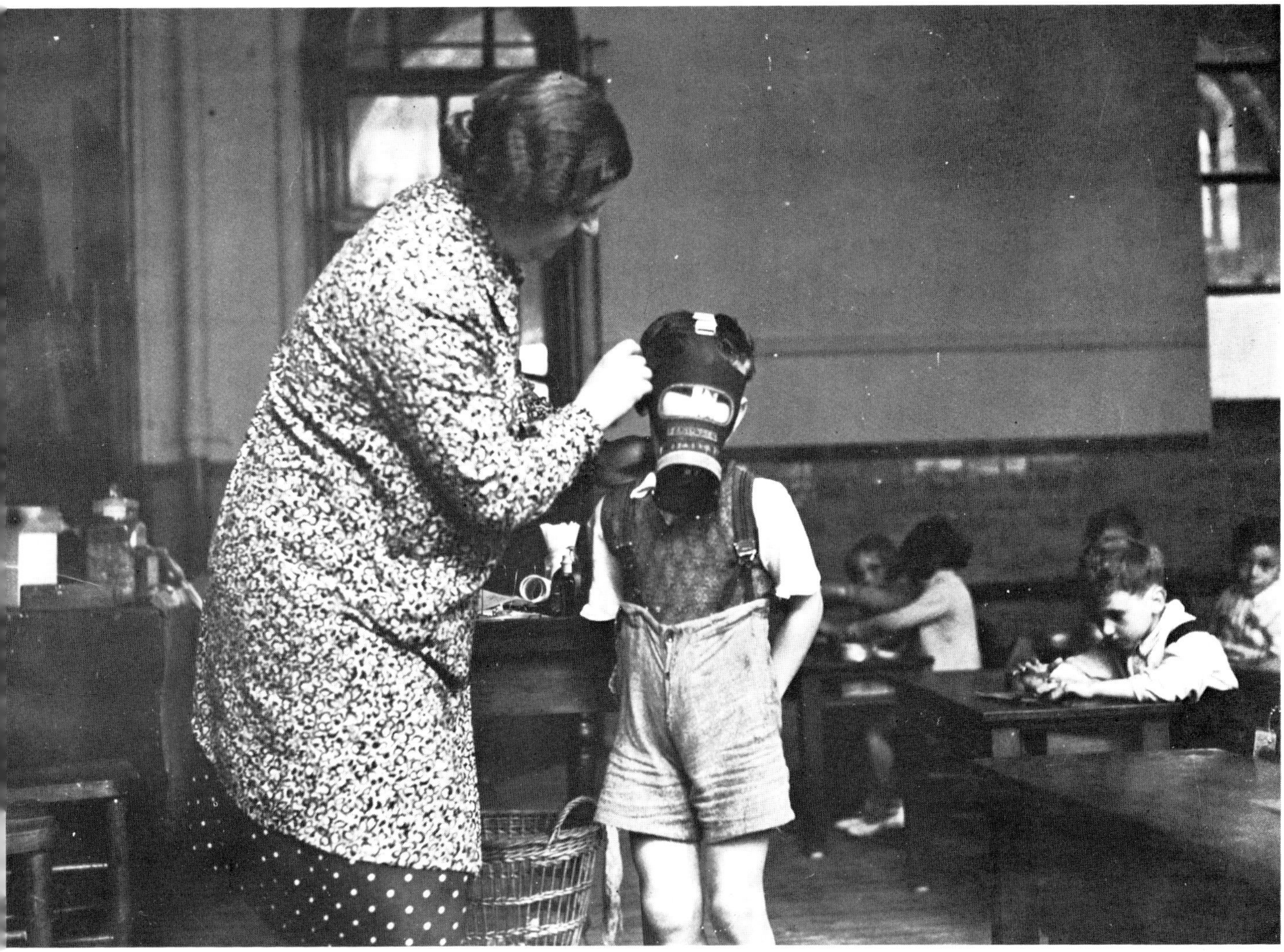

Civilians were involved from the start, for the threat of poison gas, air raids and even invasion was taken seriously. The first evacuation began in August 1939.

Far left Two small evacuees have their labels checked at a London station in 1942.

Above Children learned to use their gasmasks at school.

Left In the grounds of Westminster School, a sacrist to Westminster Abbey learns rifle drill with the home guard.

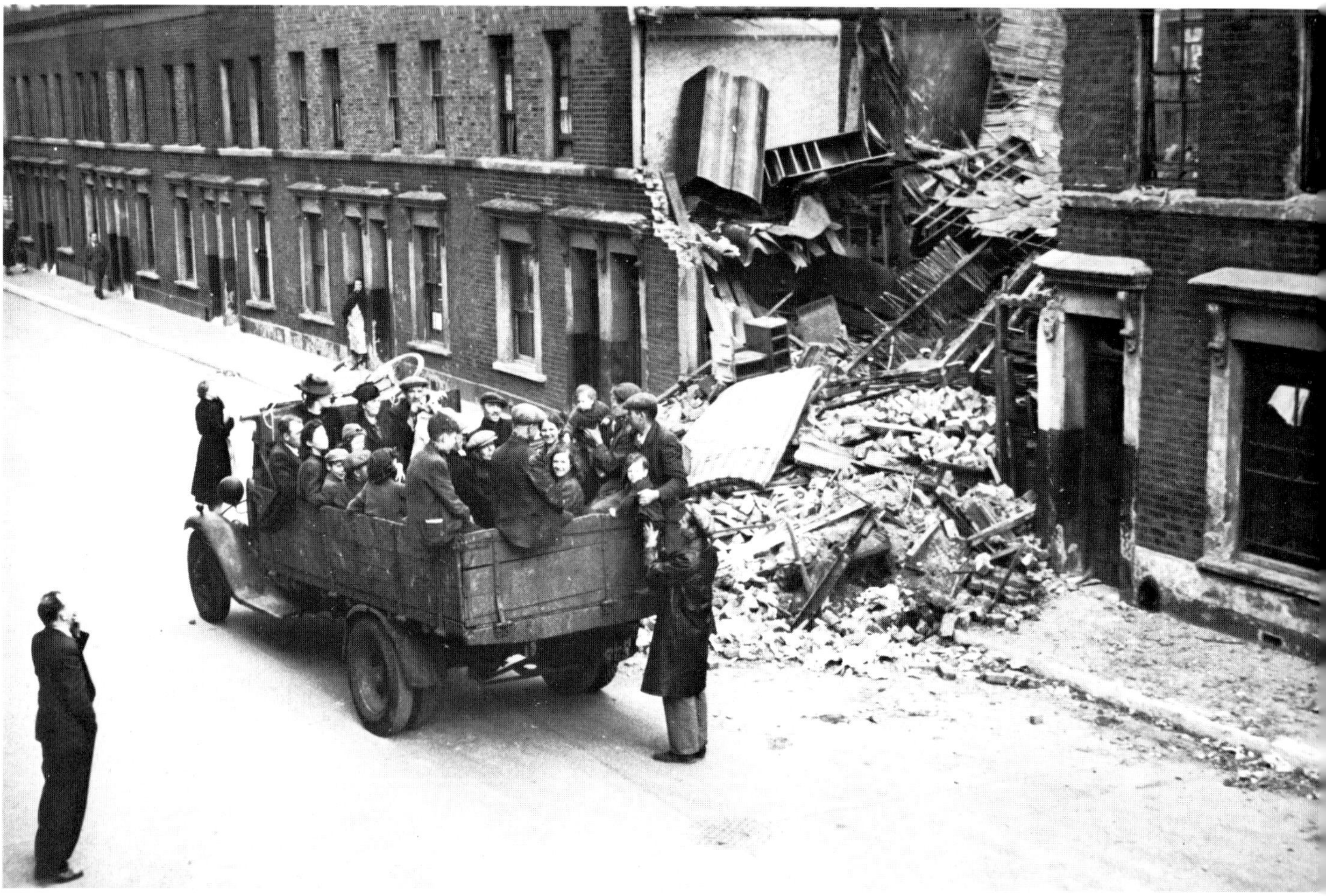

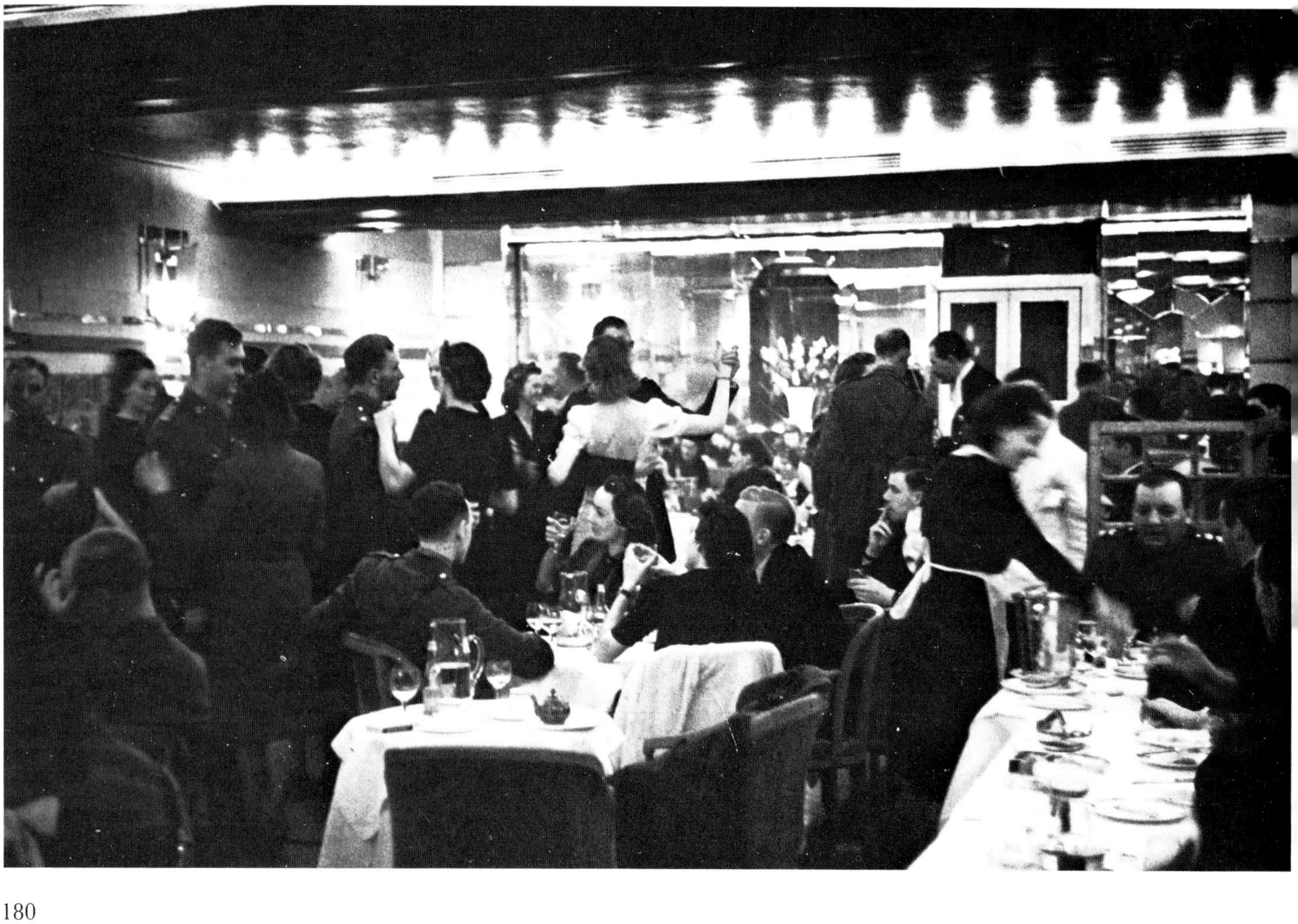

Above left A familiar sight in the East End of London during the Blitz, 1940.

Above November 14th, 1940. Coventry Cathedral in ruins.

Left Night life continues in London's West End, 1941.

Above The Kardomah Café in Fleet Street could shelter 250 people.

Above right Fire spotters helped counter the threat of incendiary bombs.

Right Piccadilly Tube Station during an air raid, 1940. Throughout London, underground stations became overnight shelters.

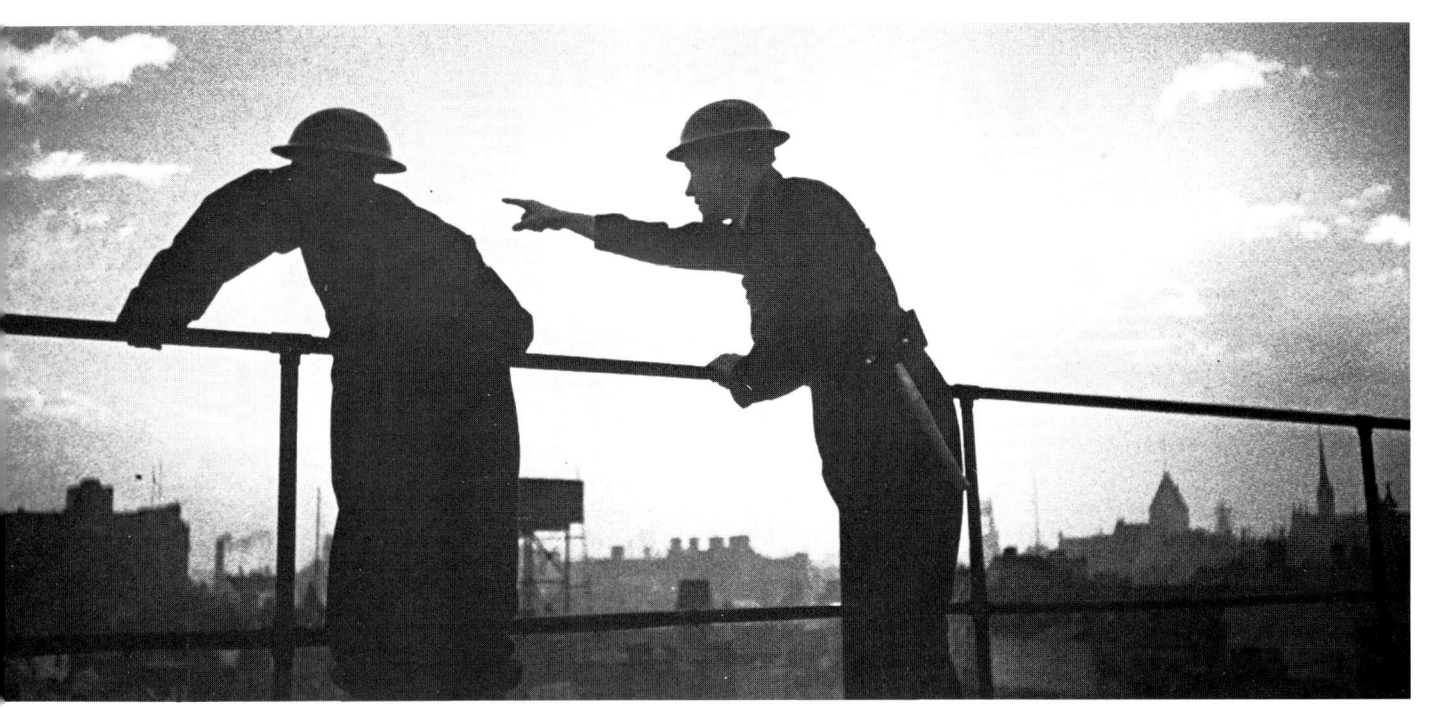

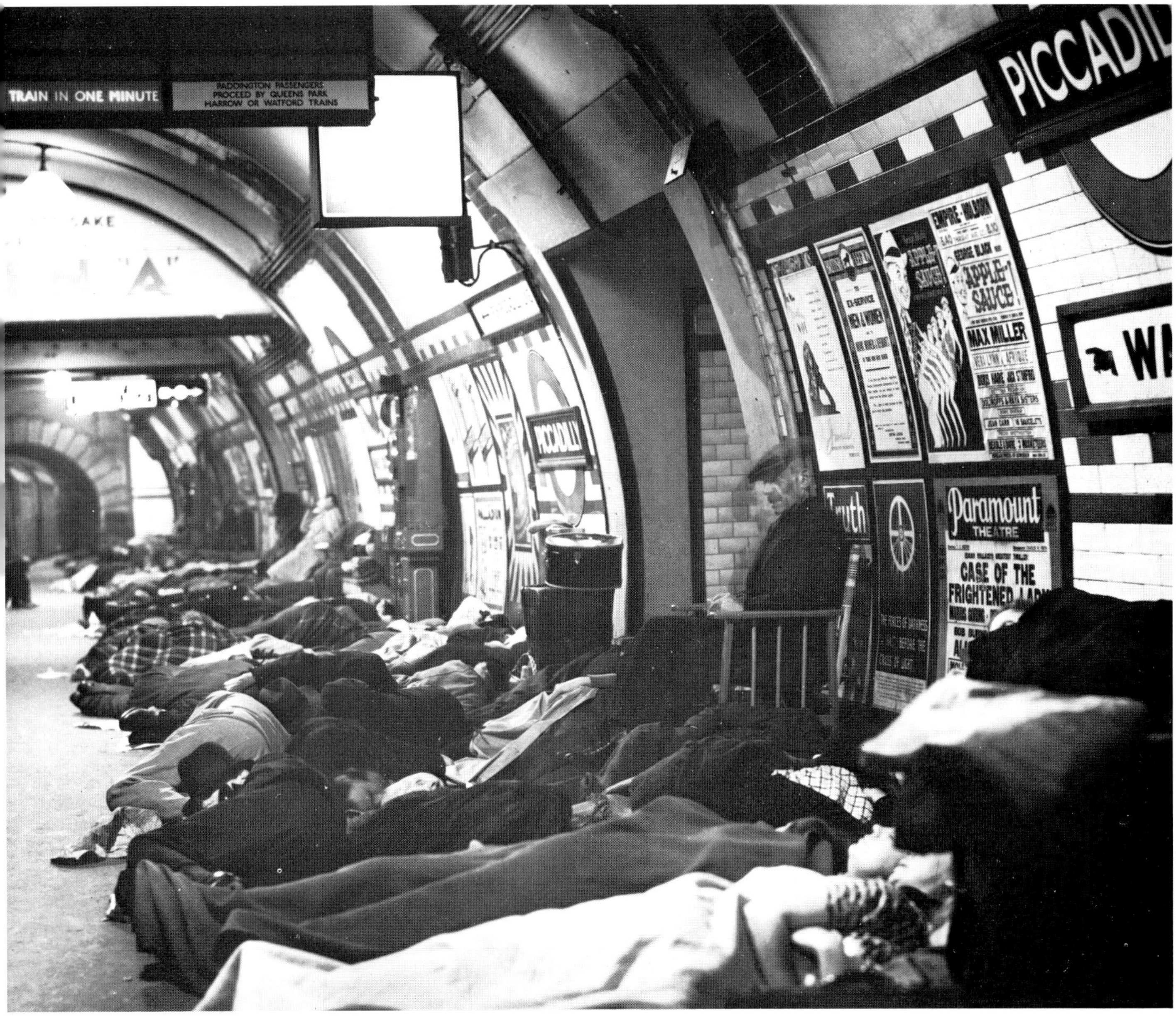
TRAIN IN ONE MINUTE
PADDINGTON PASSENGERS
PROCEED BY QUEENS PARK
HARROW OR WATFORD TRAINS
PICCADIL
PICCADILLY
EX-SERVICE
MEN & WOMEN
EMPIRE · HOLBORN
GEORGE BLACK
APPLE-SAUCE!
MAX MILLER
Truth
Paramount
THEATRE
CASE OF THE
FRIGHTENED LA

VE Day celebrations in London, May 8th 1945. The war in Europe was over.

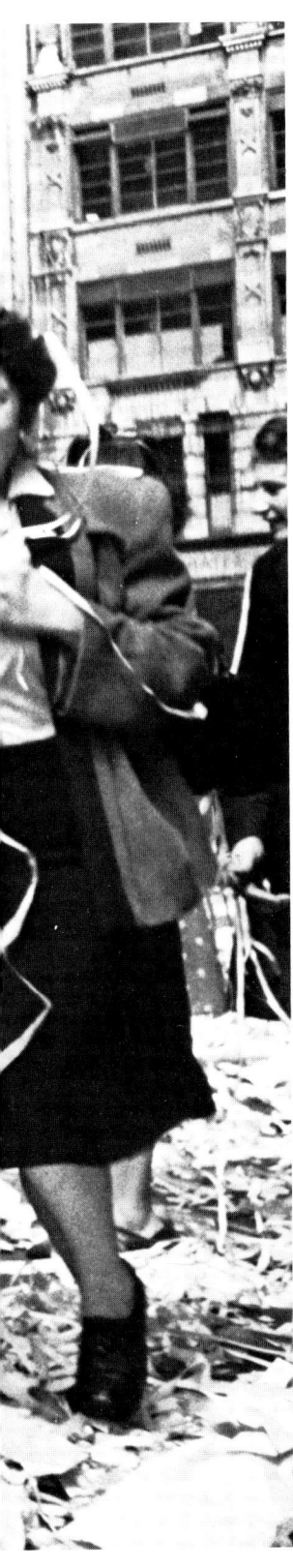

185

Body and Soul

The hospitals and schools available to the public in 1856 were mostly charitable institutions, poorly equipped and badly run.

Above Florence Nightingale in 1855. She opened the first school for nurses in 1860, after her pioneering work in the Crimea.

Right Working-class children receive free education at the Rev. Thomas Guthrie's Ragged School in Edinburgh in 1857.

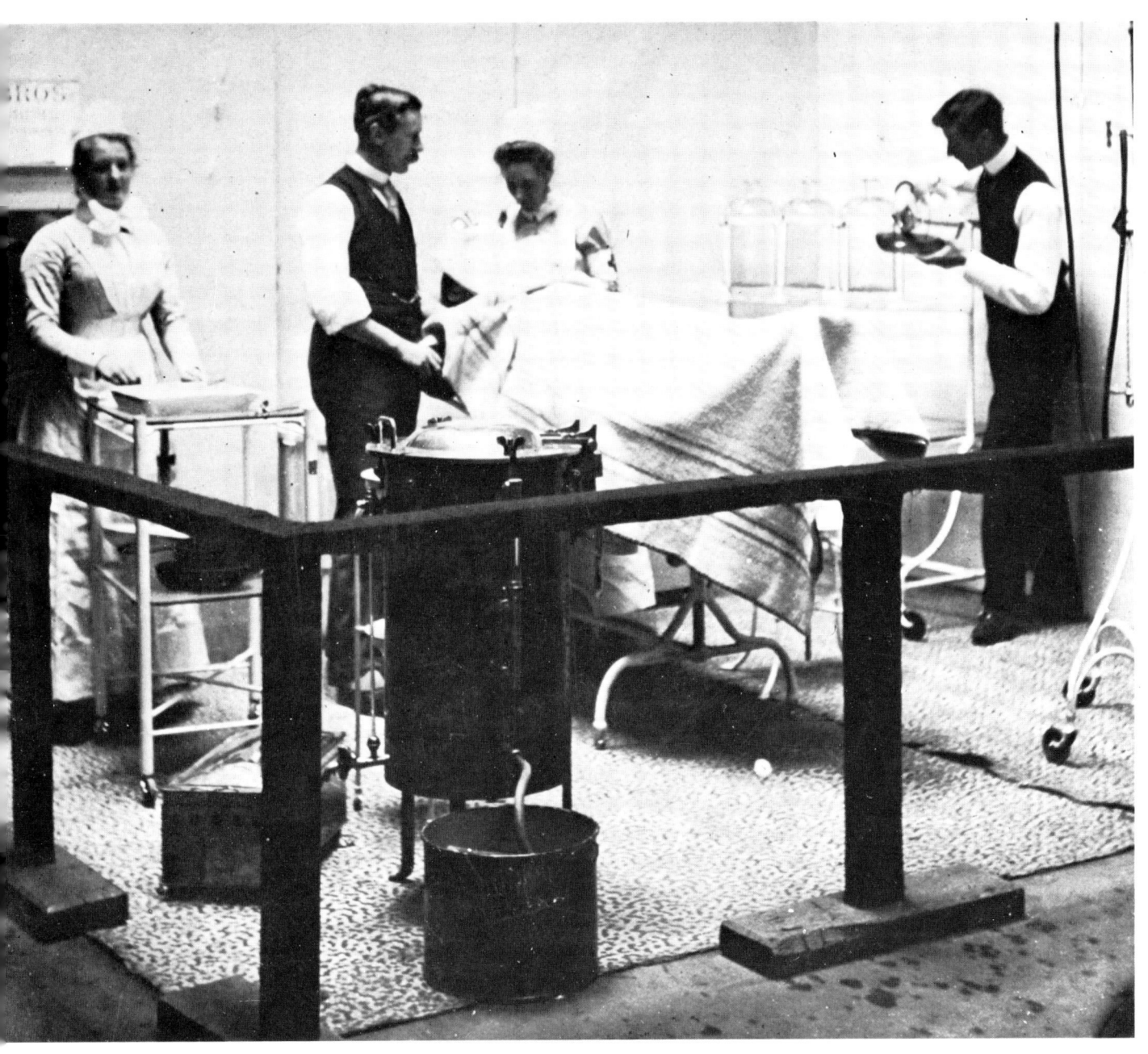

Left A street pedlar in 1870 displays his range of instant cures.

Above A model of an 1890 operating theatre showing the earliest sterilizing equipment.

Above A church baptism in 1860 — the first step in a Christian's life.

Right An open-air preacher in 1901 taking religion to the people.

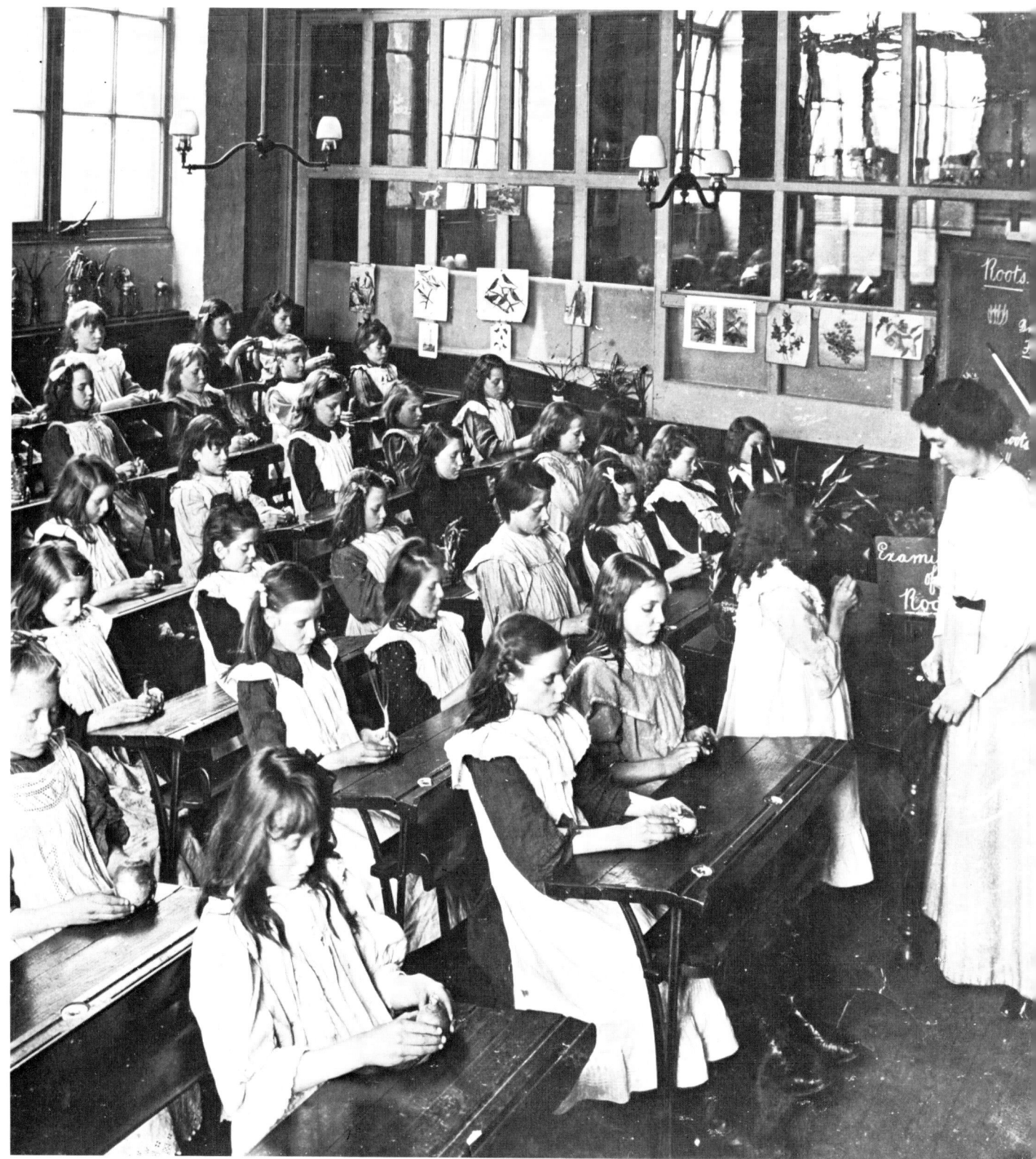

Above Nature study class in a girls elementary school in 1908.

By 1902 free and and compulsory education was provided for all children between the ages of five and twelve.

Above right London schoolboys on strike at Shoreditch in September 1911 over the use of corporal punishment.

Right Flowers for buttonholes on Founders Day at Eton — the fourth of June, 1907.

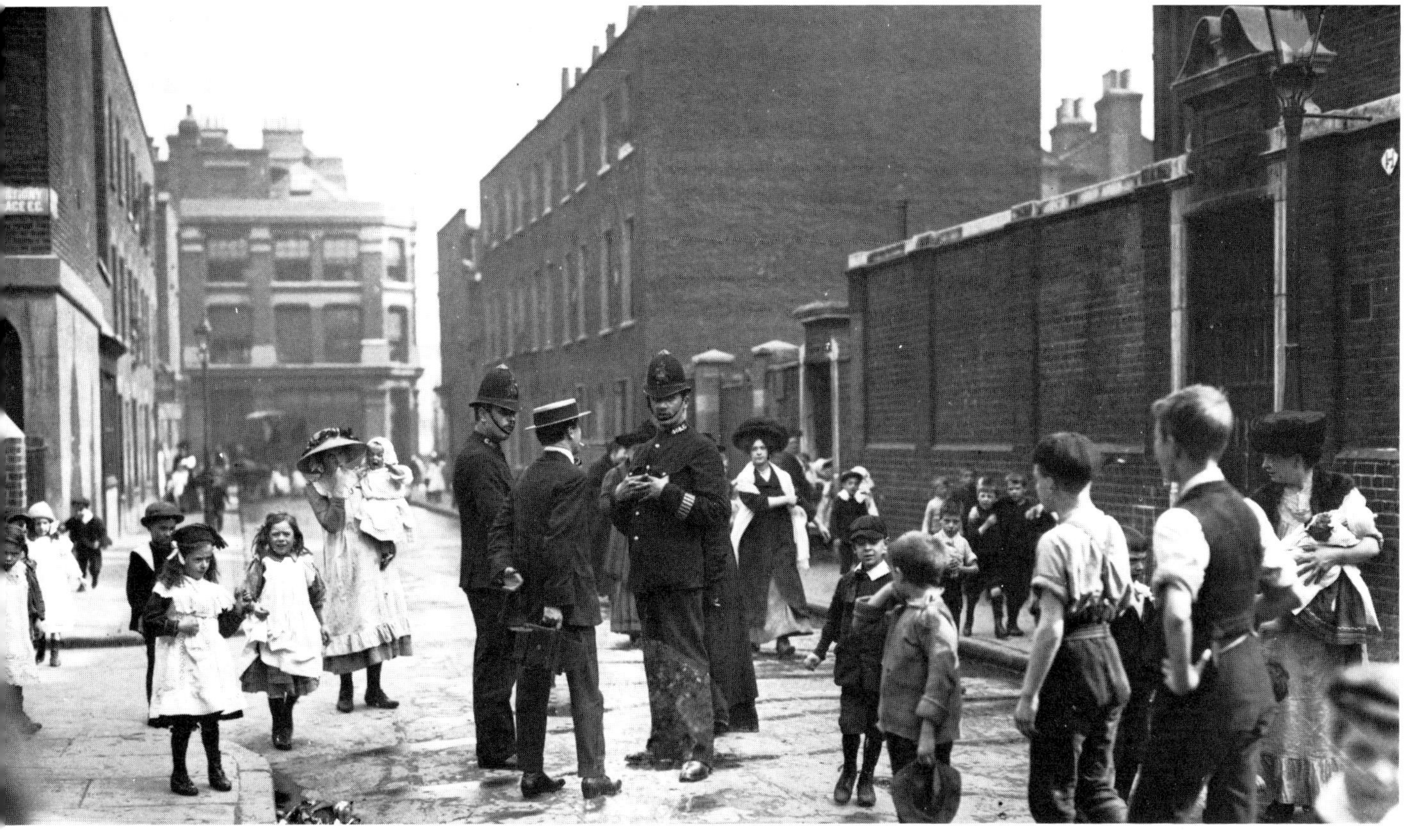

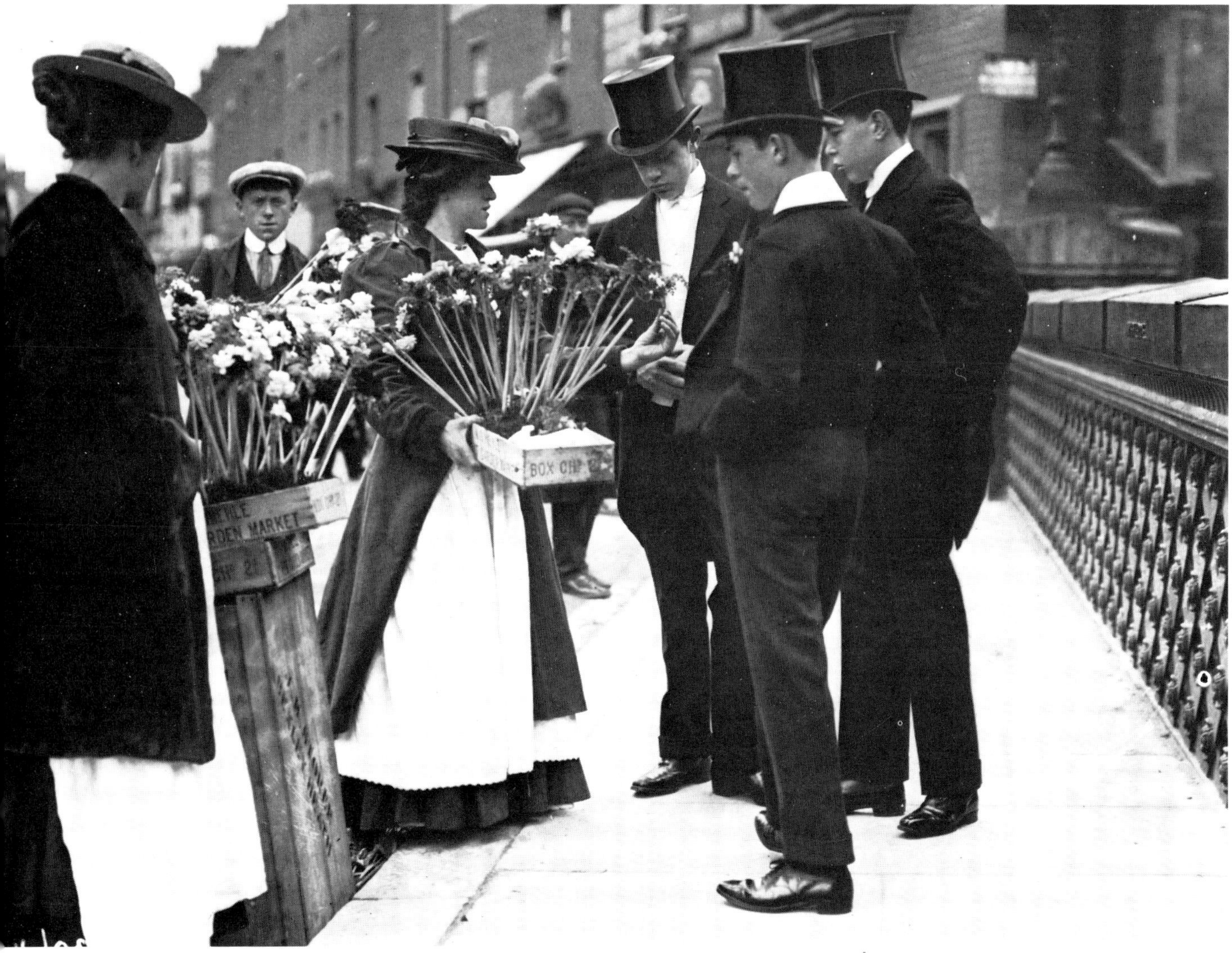

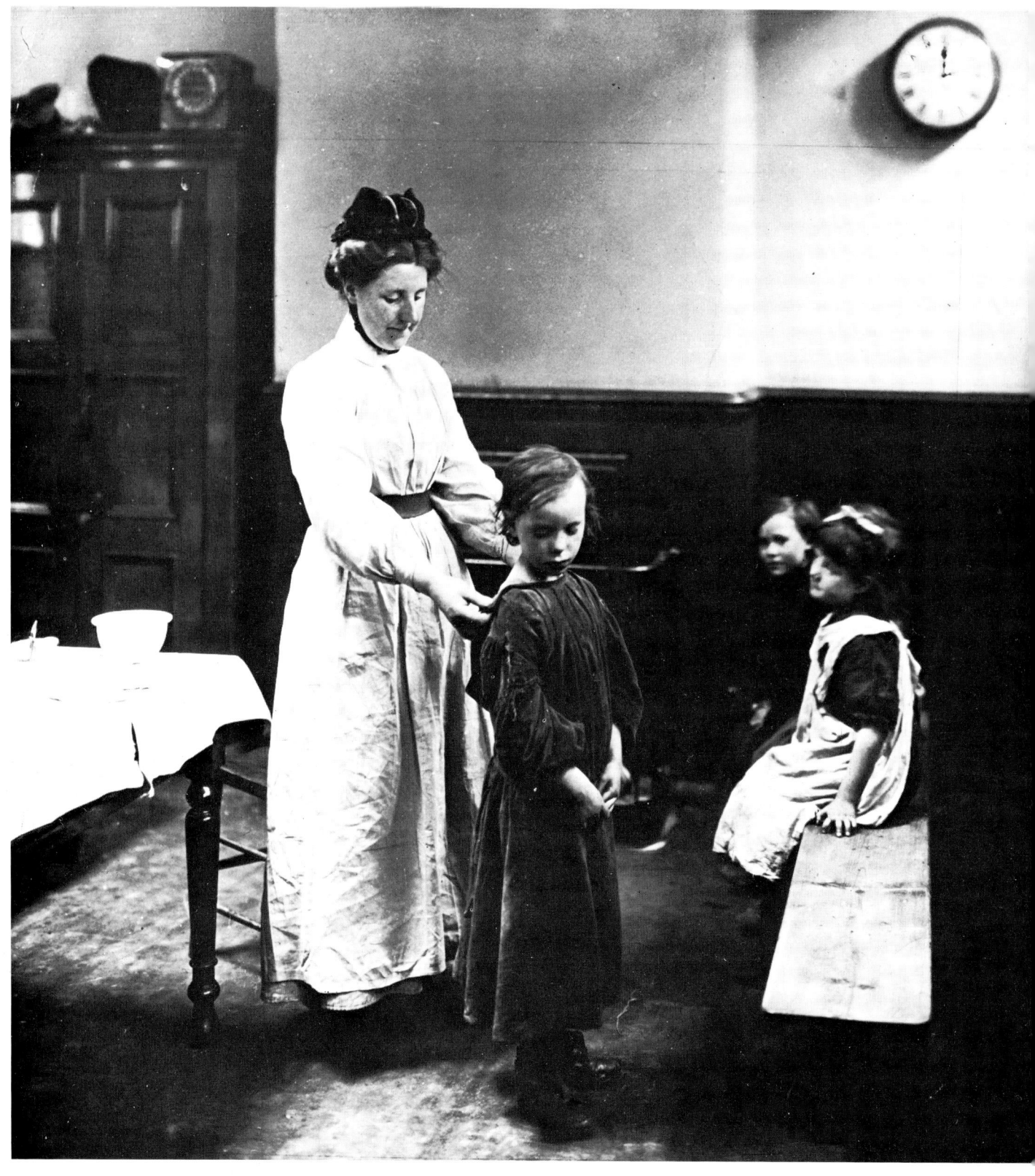

Above A medical inspection for a London child in 1912.

Above right Girls learning 'Mothercraft' at a day nursery in Acton in 1912.

Right A Red Cross motor ambulance crew in action in 1928.

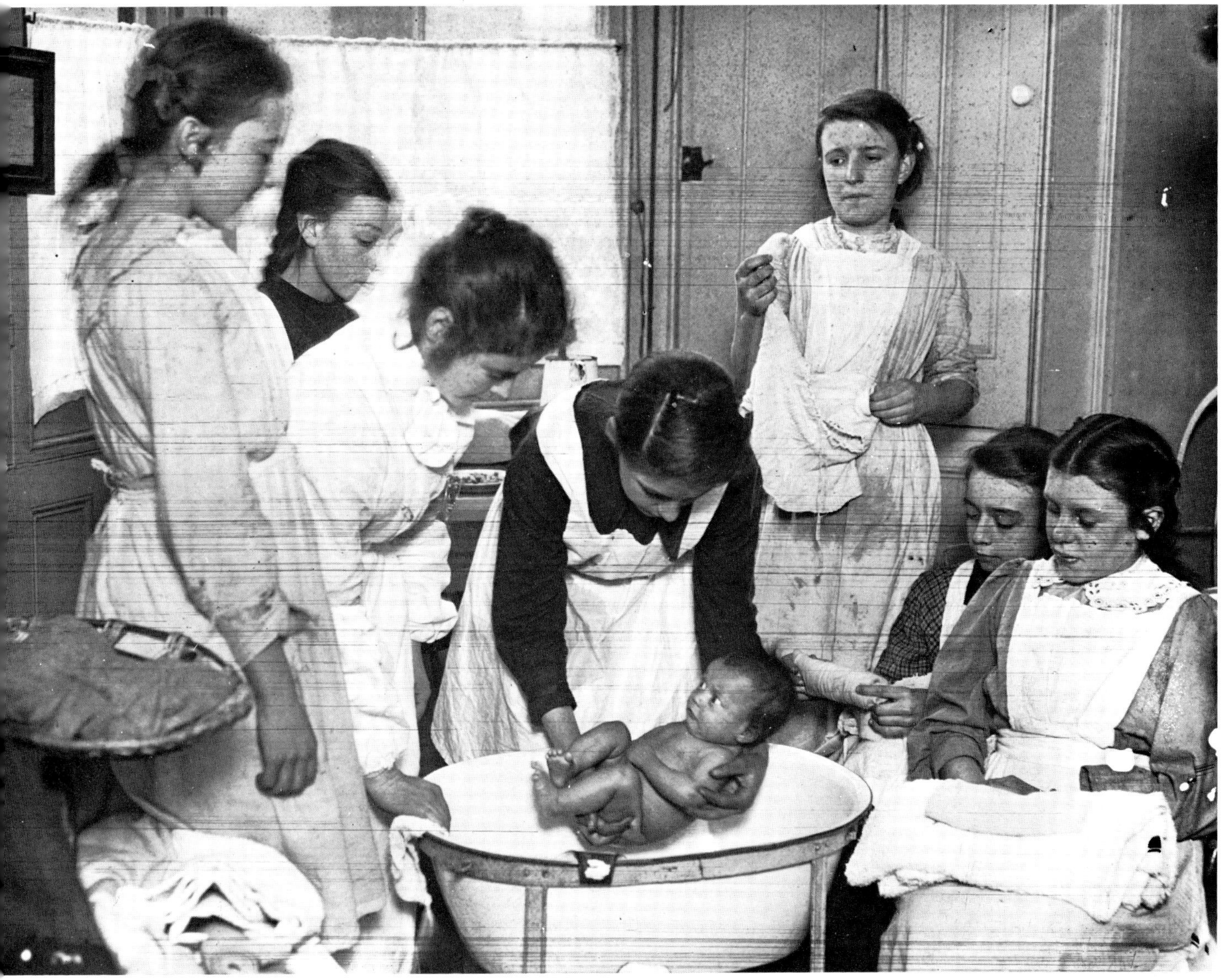

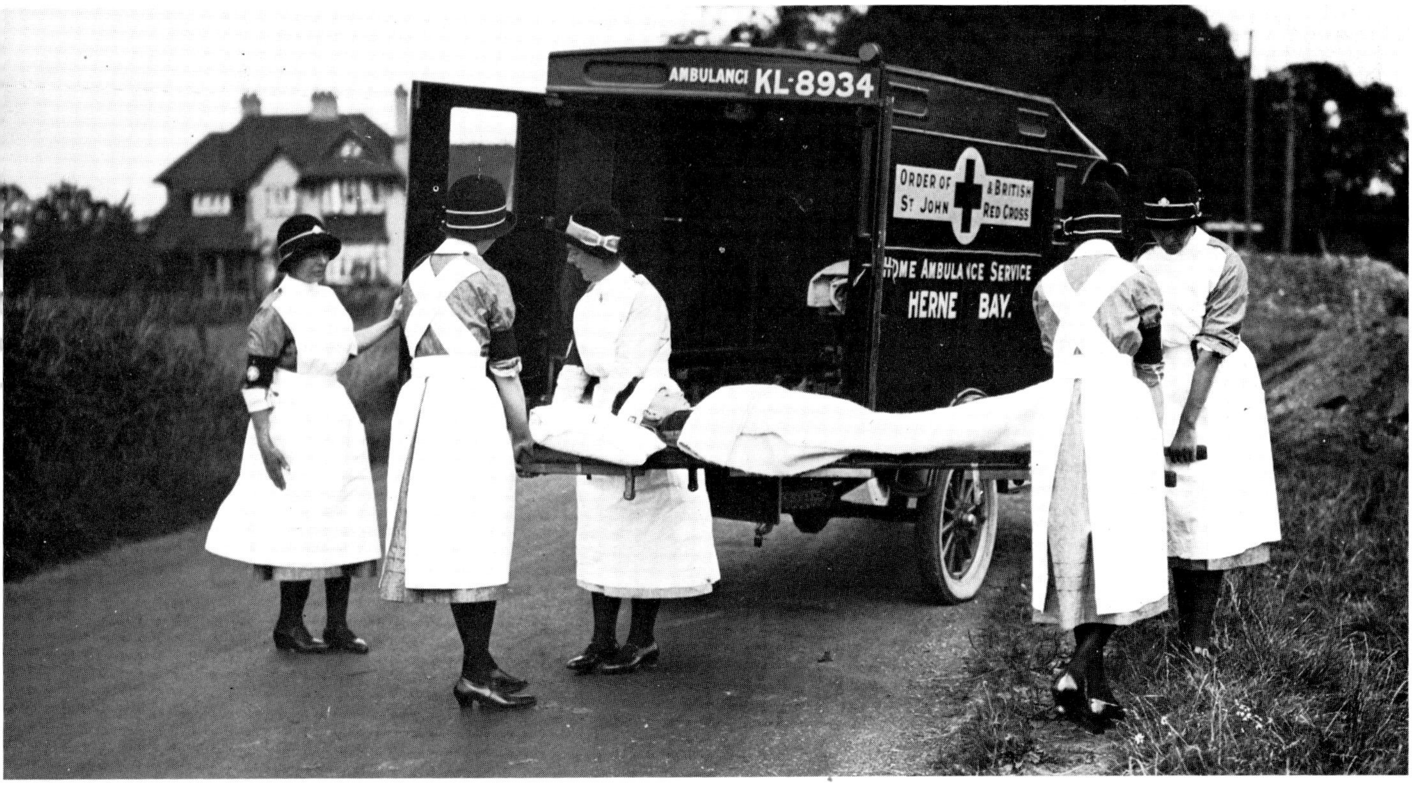
AMBULANCI KL-8934
ORDER OF ST JOHN
& BRITISH RED CROSS
HOME AMBULANCE SERVICE
HERNE BAY.

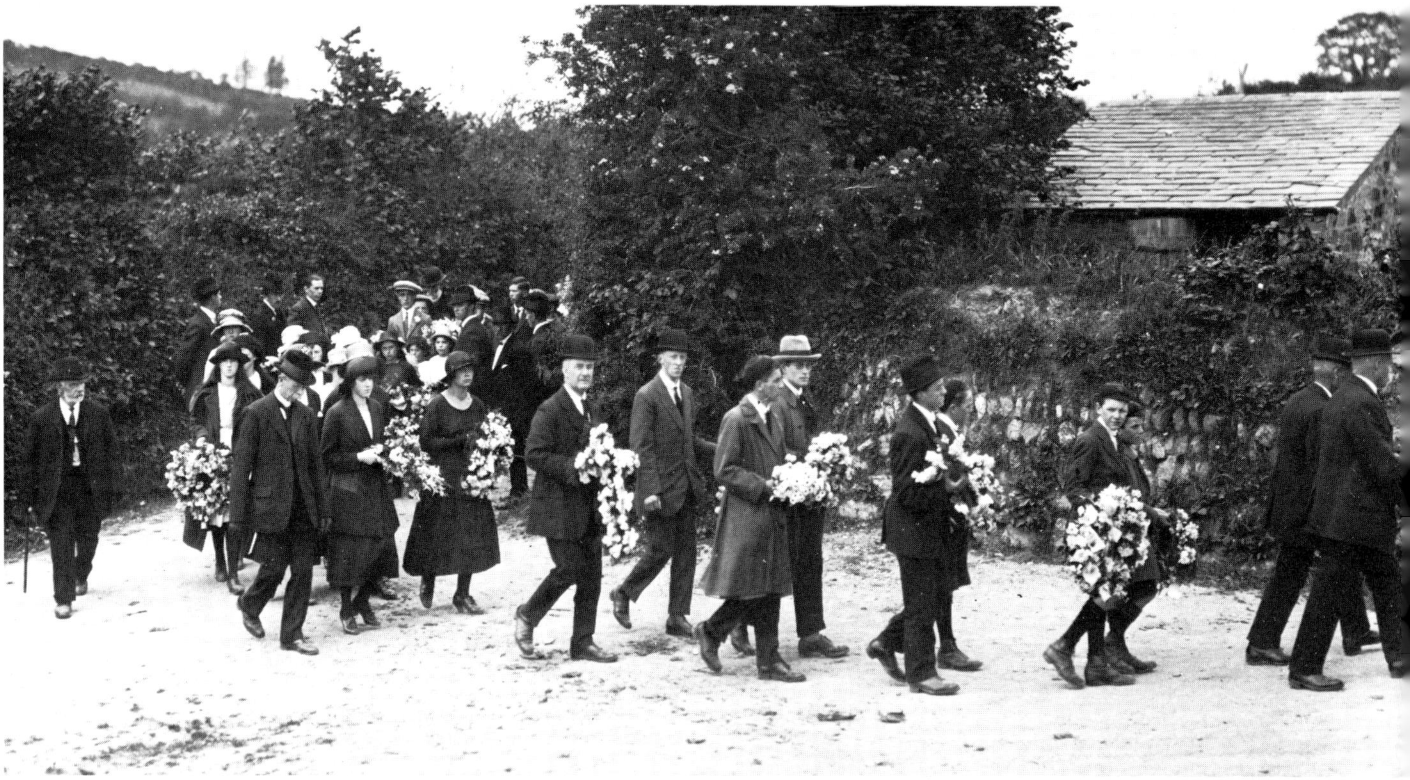

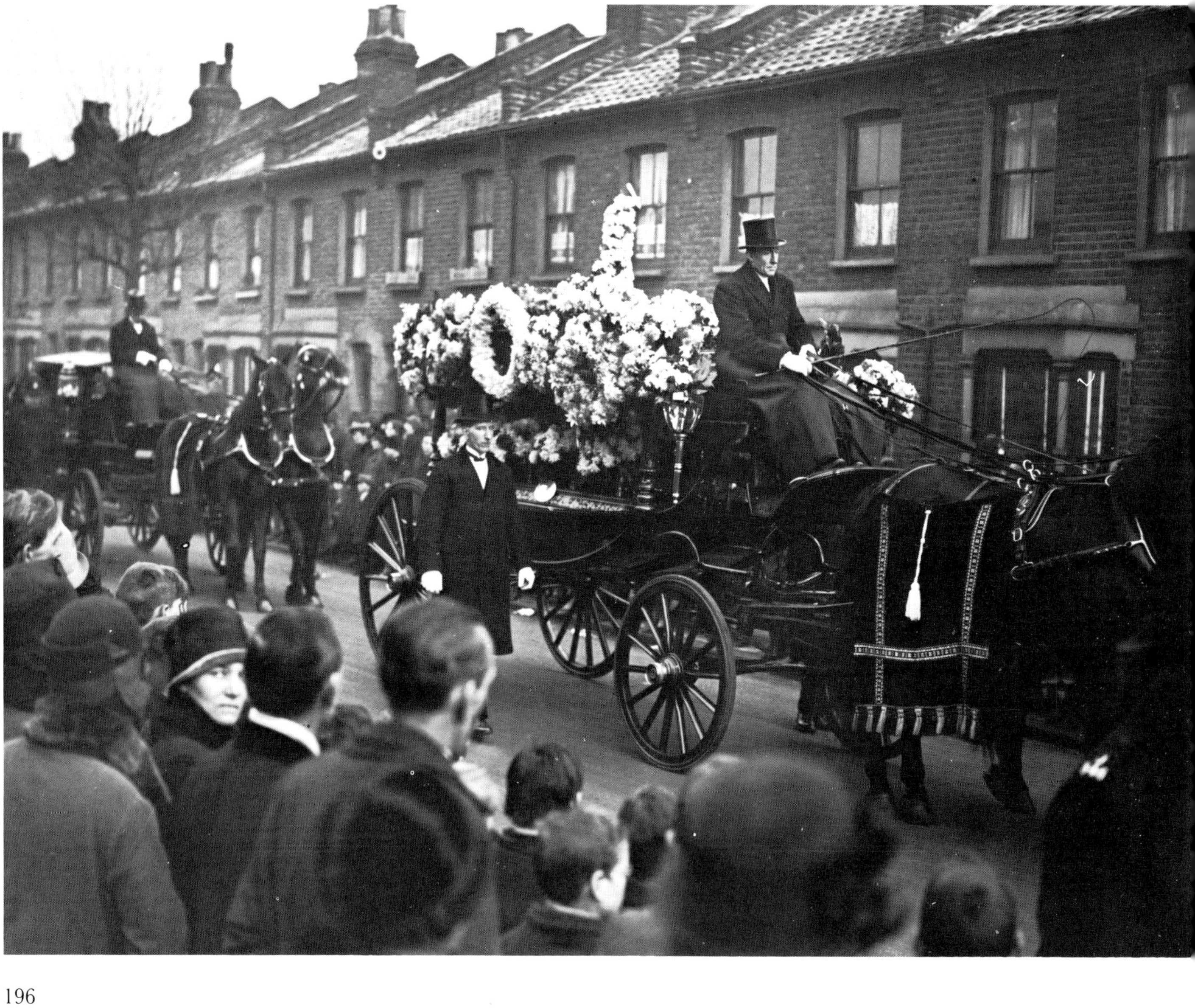

Above A wedding at Ivybridge in Devon, 1925.

Above left Wreaths at the funeral of Edith Parkyn, murdered at Bodmin in June, 1922.

Left A funeral cortège at Clapton Park in London, 1927.

Above Llansamlet, Swansea, schoolchildren in 1944.

Right The art of football — Poole's Park School, London, in 1937.

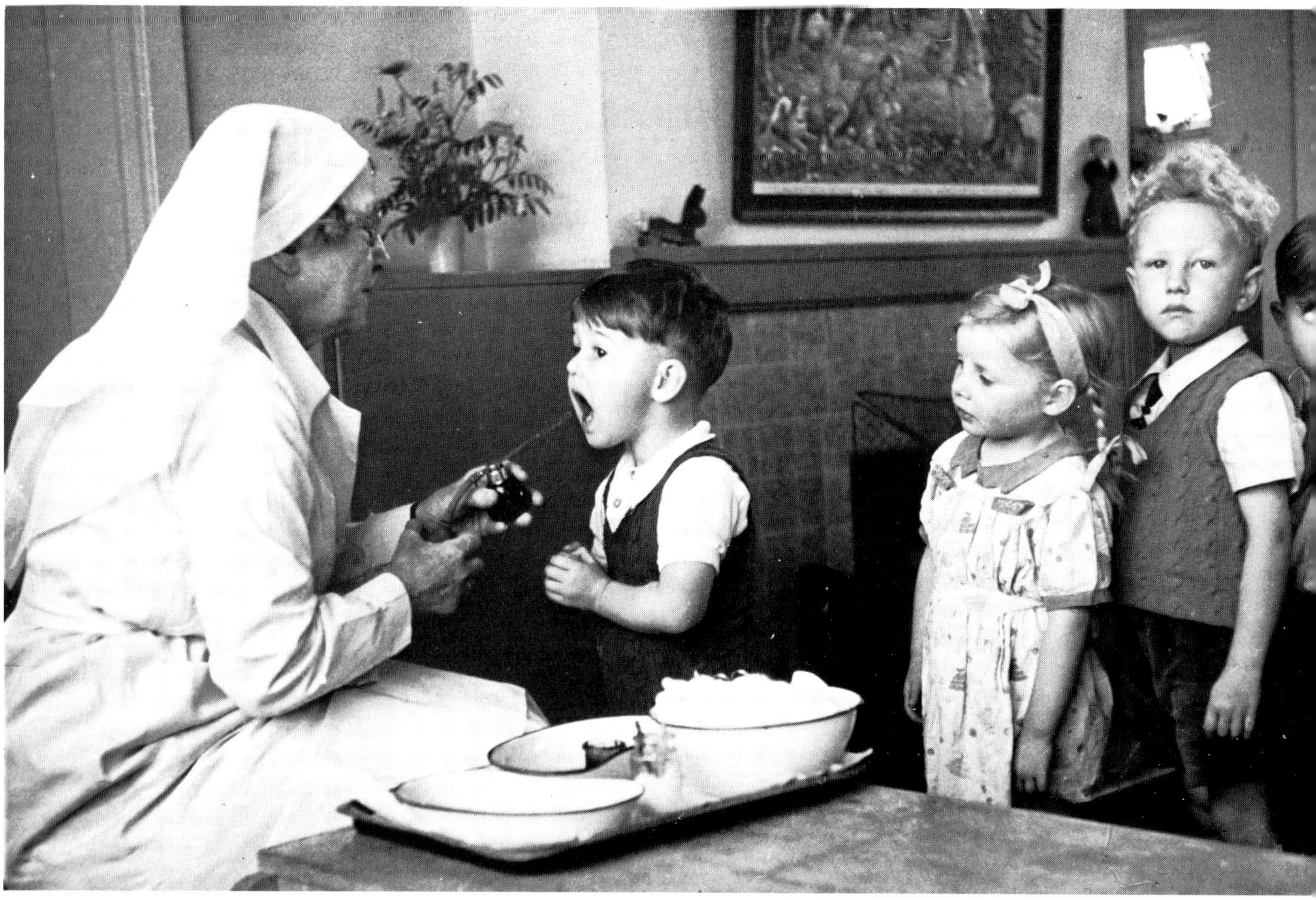

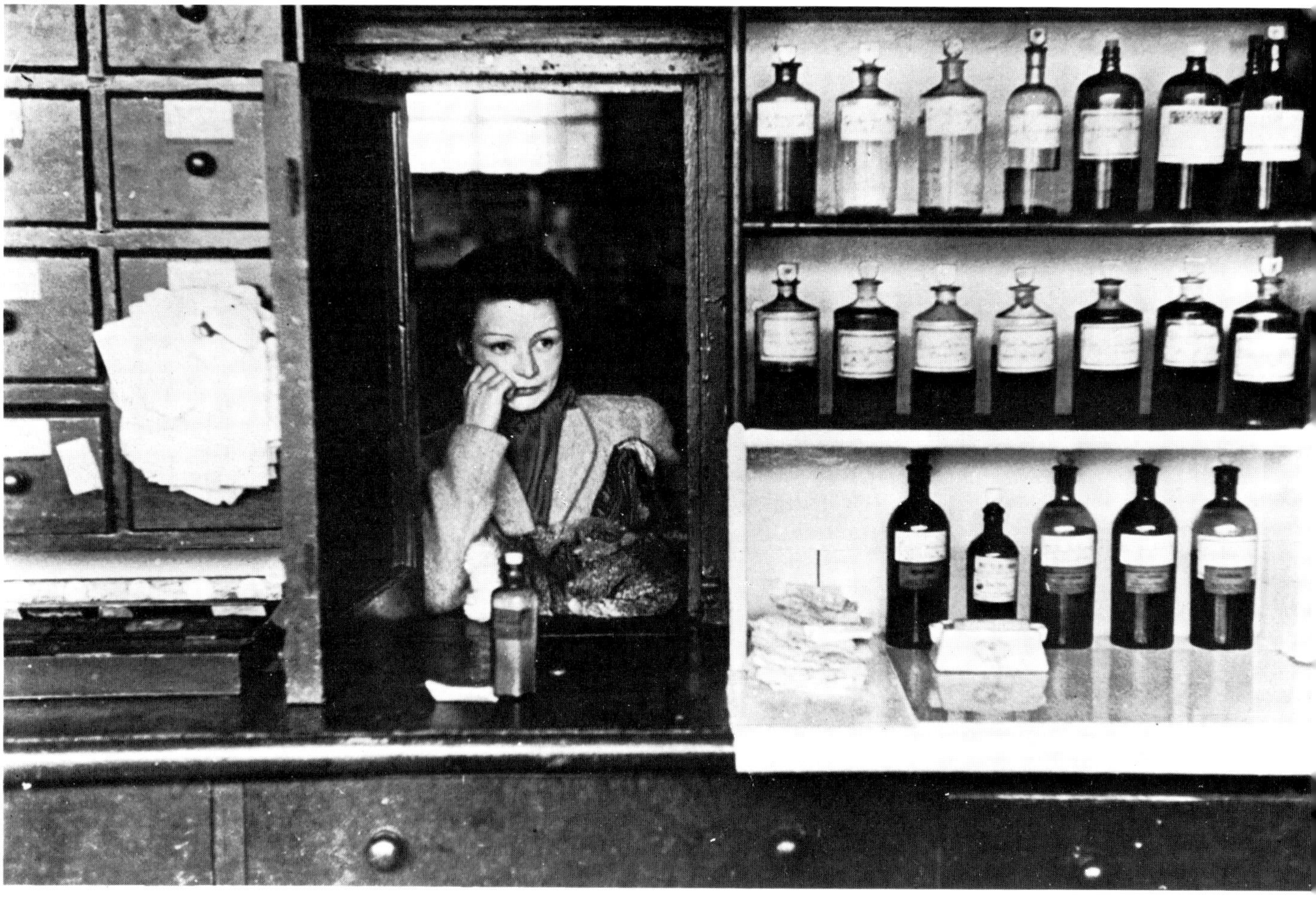

Above left Nursery school children queue for a mouth spray, 1944.

Above Hygiene in the operating theatre.

Left Waiting for a prescription at the Tredegar Health Centre in Monmouthshire in April 1946 just before the establishment of the National Health Service.

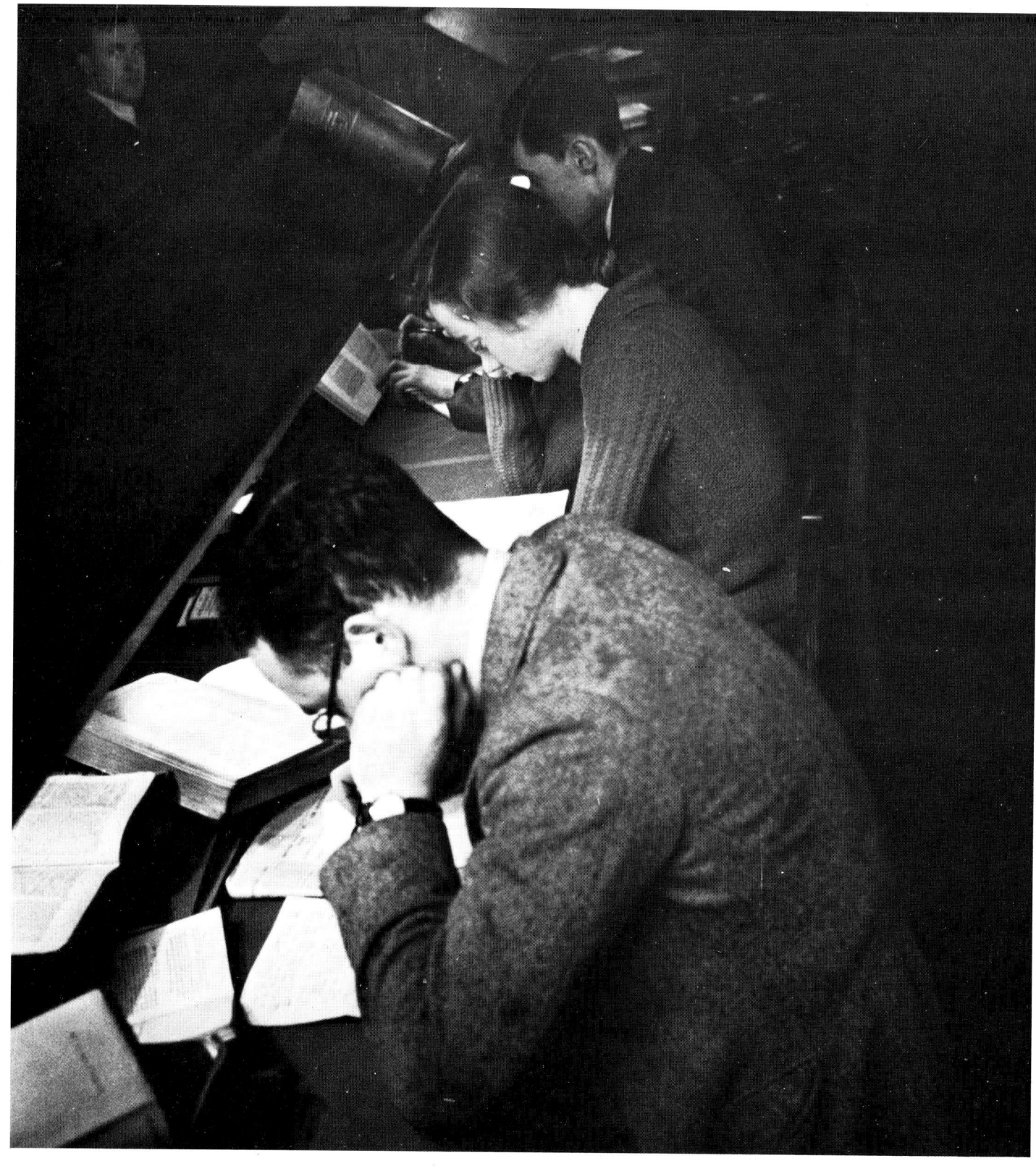

By 1956, secondary education was compulsory for all and there were 90,000 students at British universities.

Above Preparation for exams at the London School of Economics.

Above right Morning prayers at the village school of Westerleigh, near Bristol, in 1953.

Right End of term at the Hugh Myddleton School, London, in 1931.

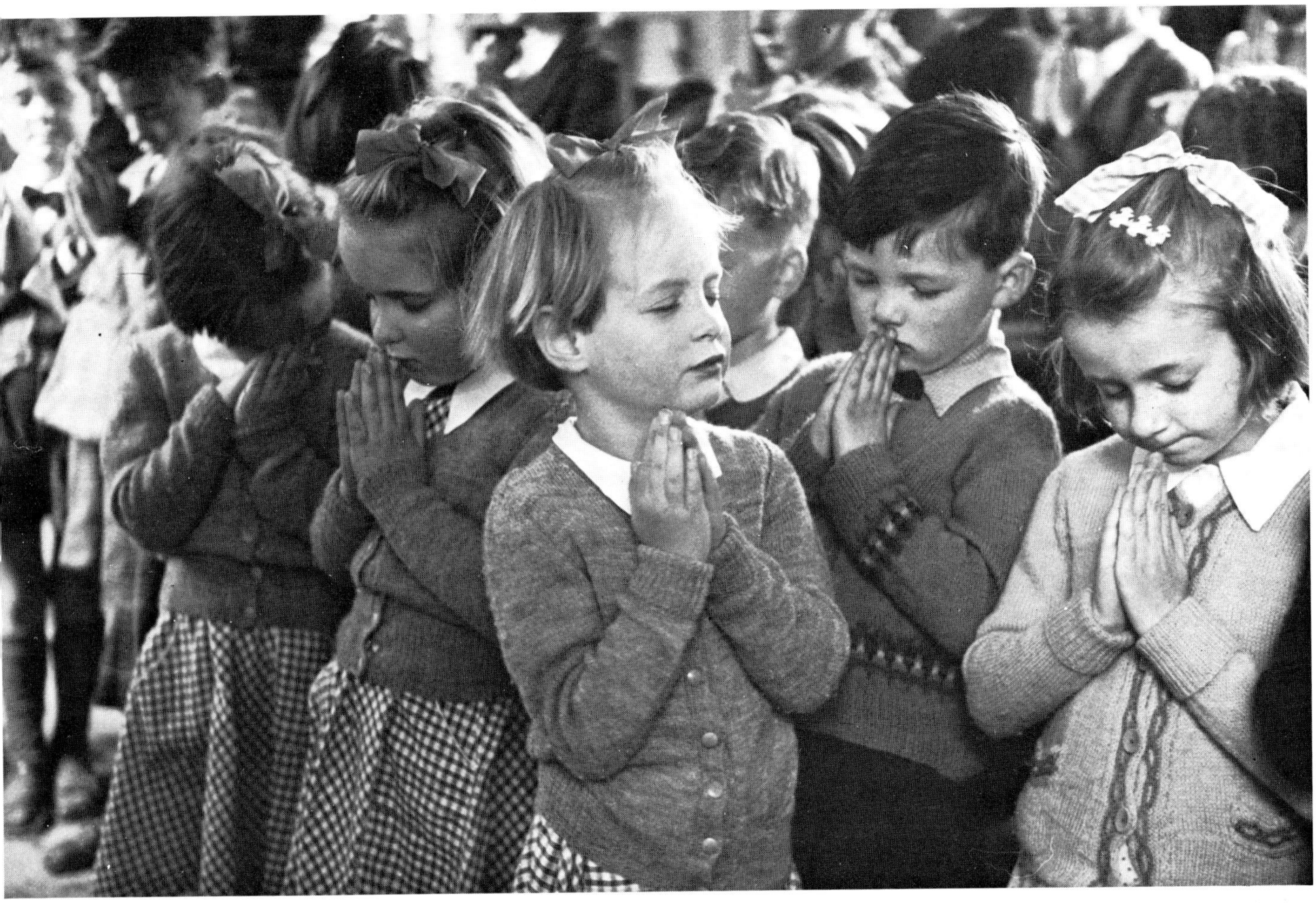

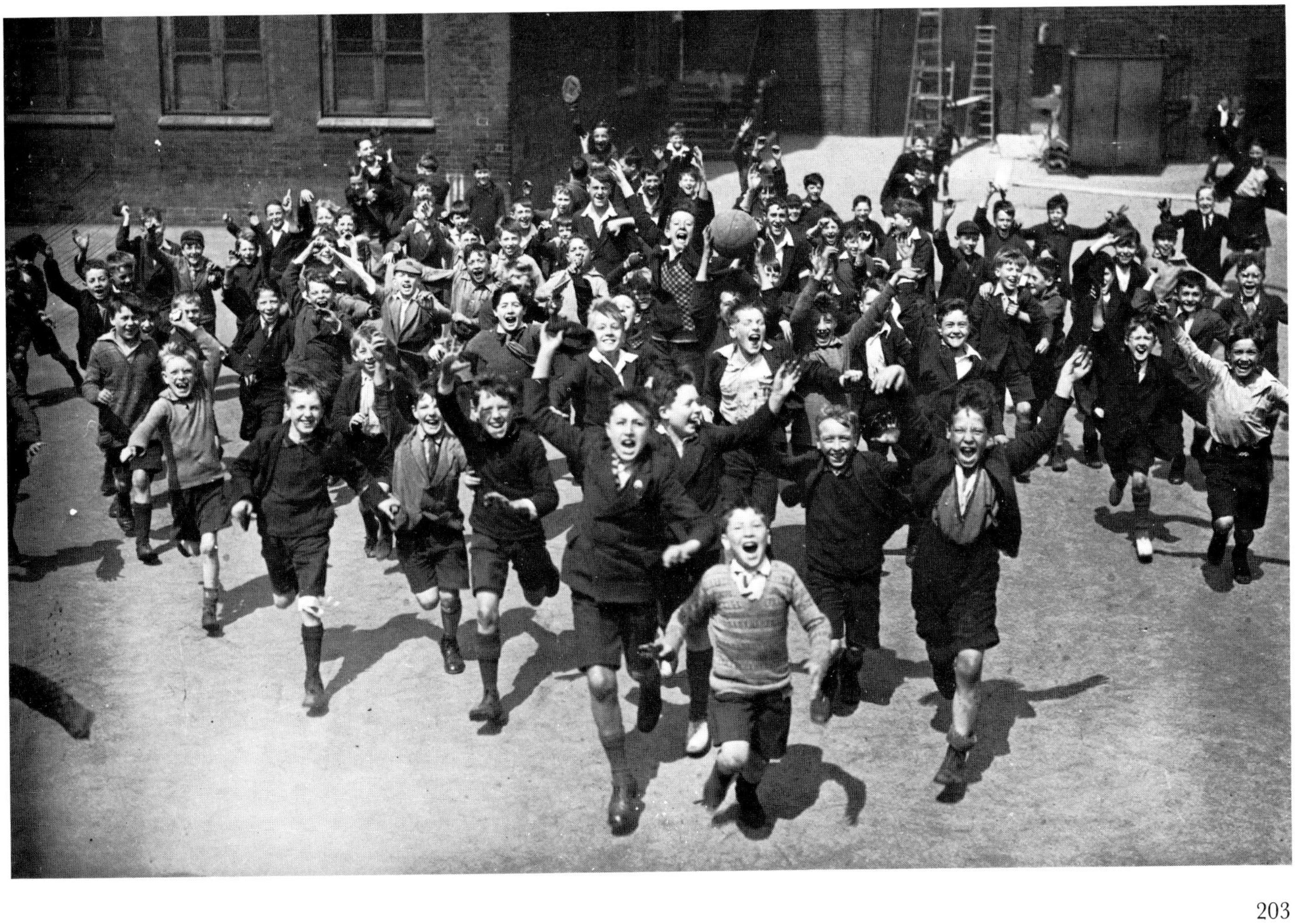

Entertainment

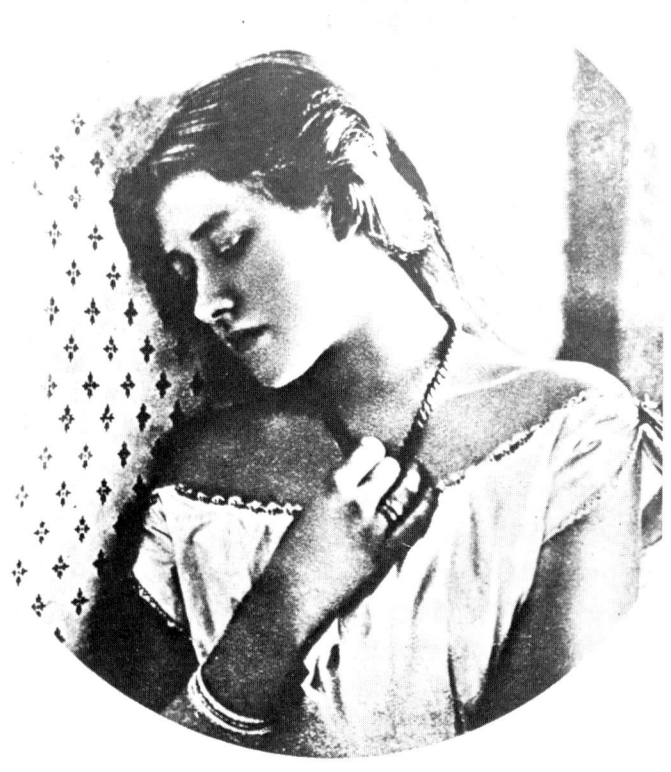

Theatre was one of the few entertainments patronized by the Victorian middle class. The repertory was taken mainly from the classics.

Above A remarkable portrait of Ellen Terry (by Julia Margaret Cameron) in 1865 when she was only 17.

Right Lillie Langtry appearing as Cleopatra in an 1890 production of *Anthony and Cleopatra* at the Princes Theatre. She hired the theatre especially for the production.

Above A scene from an 1880s production of the Gilbert and Sullivan opera, *Patience.*

Right A concert party in 1884 with the Nigger minstrel of Eastbourne.

Right Ellen Terry in 1896,
appearing as Imogen in
Shakespeare's *Cymbeline*.

Far right A matinee audience at
London's Haymarket Theatre in
1899.

Above The queue for the last performance of *Chu Chin Chow* at His Majesty's Theatre in 1921 after the show's record run.

Left A street musician with his barrel organ, the same year.

Above Actors performing Shakespeare to a microphone in 1923 in one of the earliest radio broadcasts.

Above right The special Grand National train in March 1923, fitted with a wireless saloon.

Right A demonstration of the Baird Cathode-Ray Television receiver in February 1935. Alexandra Palace started broadcasting in 1936.

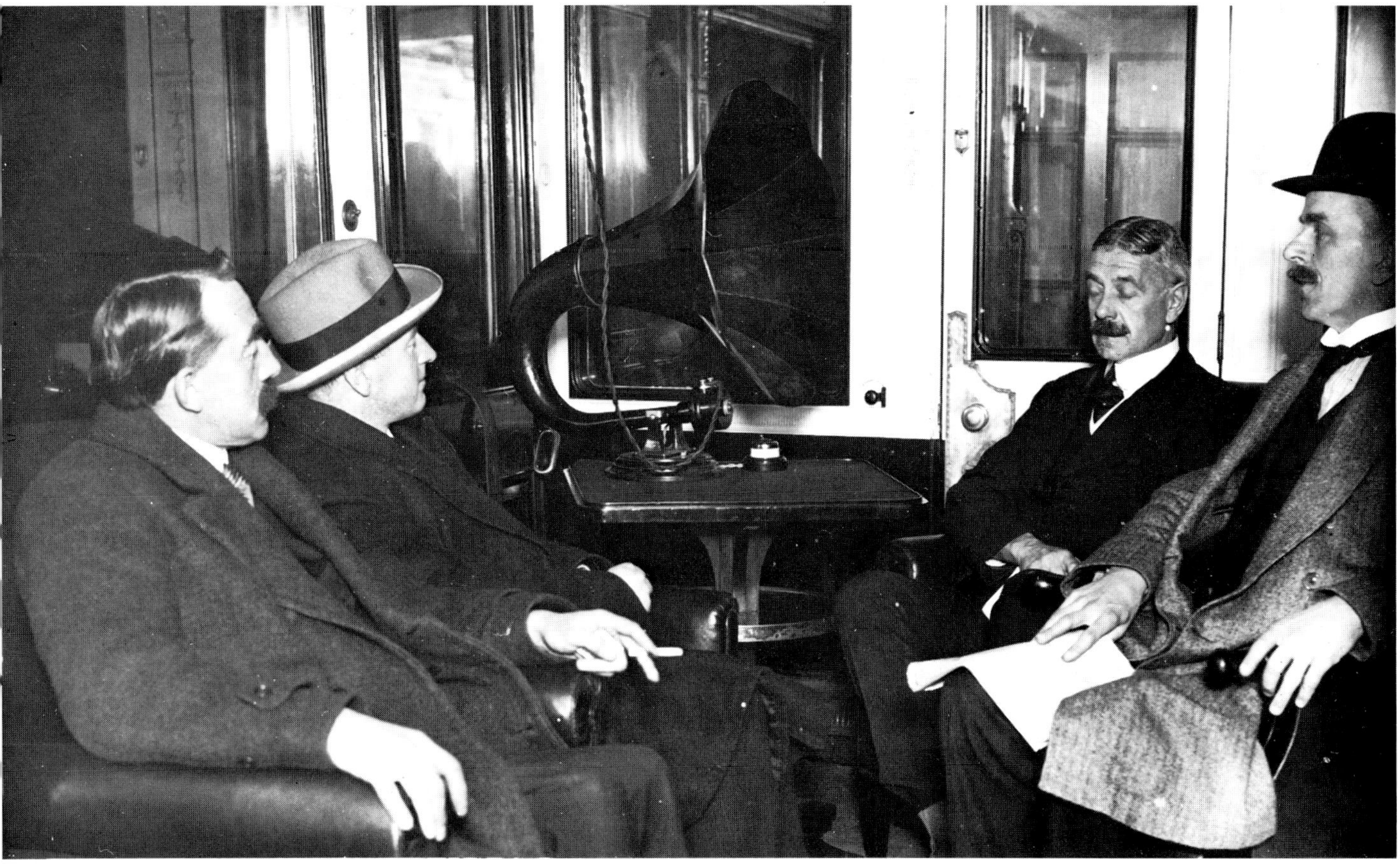

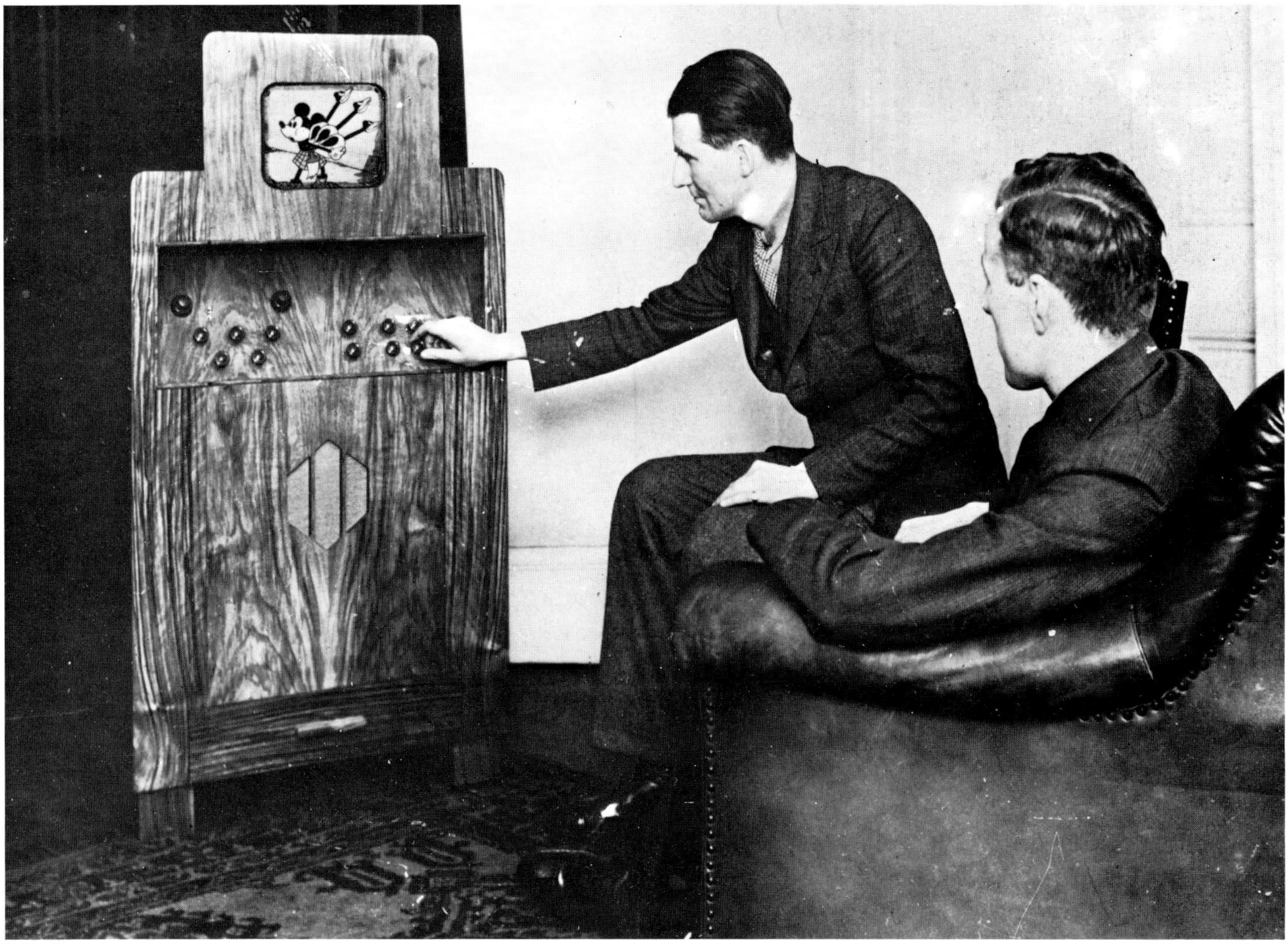

Left Spectacular costumes for the 'Shoganoff' ballet at the Princes Restaurant in 1929.

Above A costume rehearsal for the popular Ridgeway Parade revue in 1931. Although this was a radio broadcast, the costumes created the right atmosphere in the studio.

After laying the foundation stone of the new Prince of Wales Theatre in London in June 1937, Gracie Fields sings to the workmen.

Above Noel Coward and Mary Martin at a dress rehearsal for the 1947 production of *Pacific 1860.*

Above right Thomas Beecham conducting the London Philharmonic Orchestra in 1944.

Right A television preview of the Royal Academy's summer exhibition in 1939.

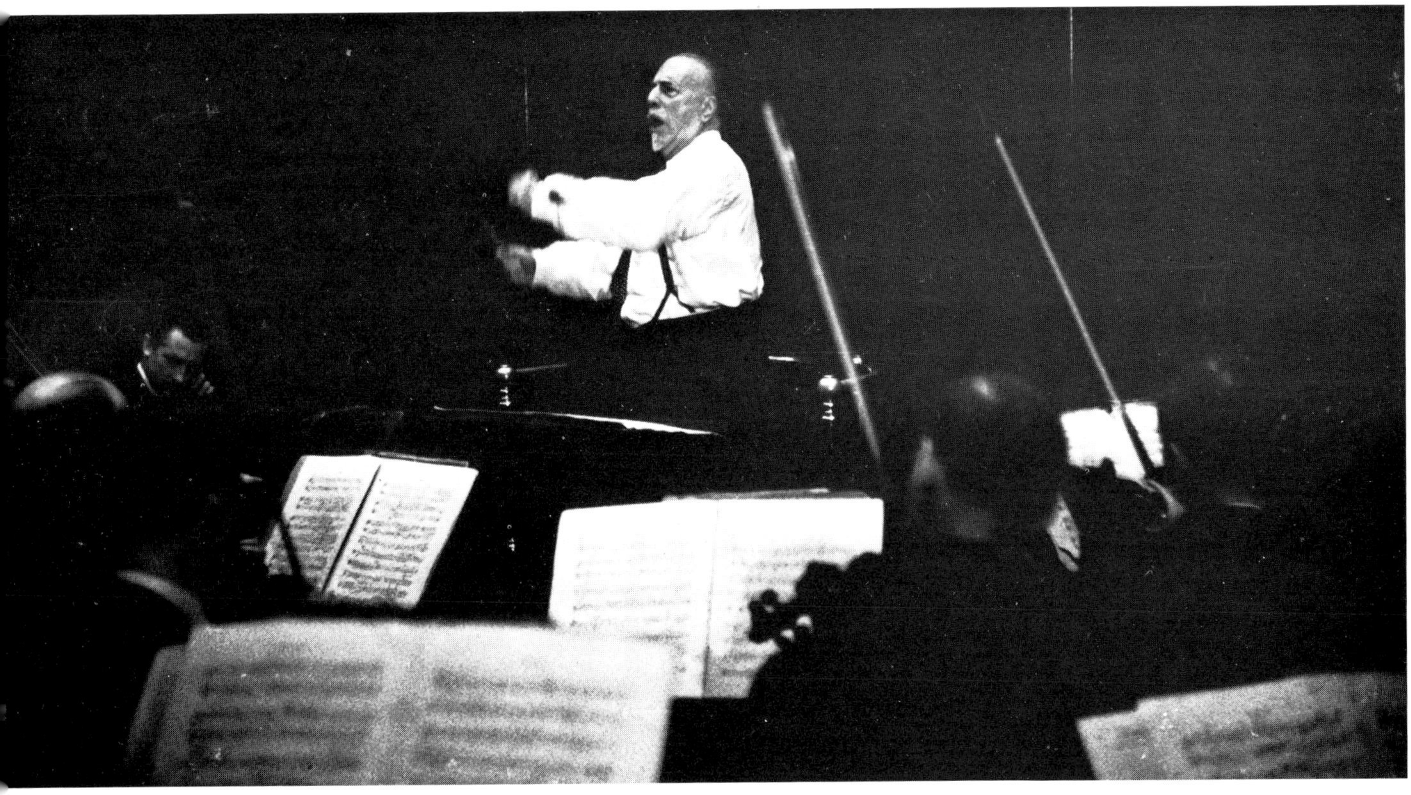

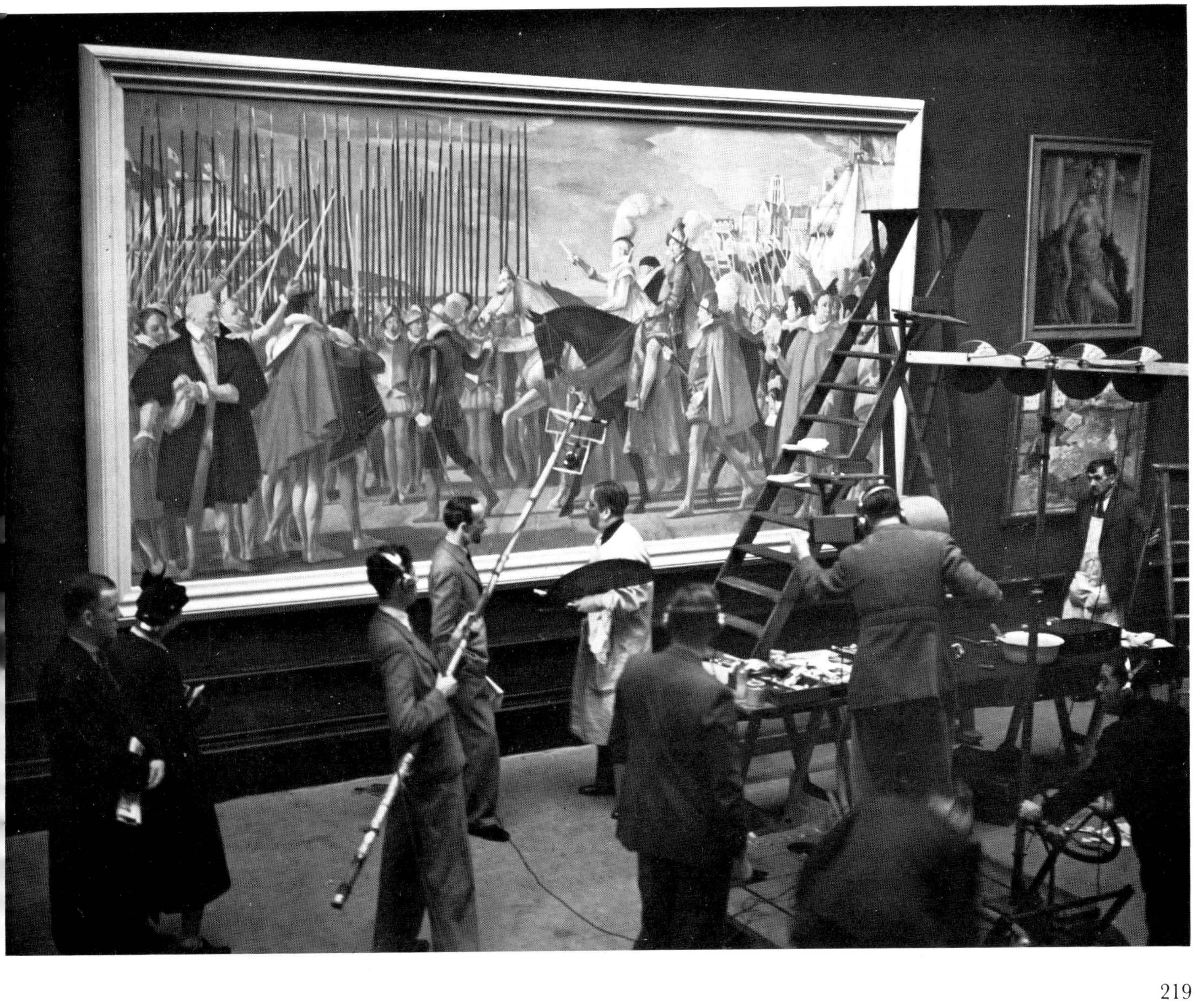

Above Peter Sellers as Groucho Marx in a Coronation year cabaret production of 'The Blue Bird' at the Pigalle Restaurant in Piccadilly, 1953.

Right Alec Guiness being made up as Fagin for the 1948 film version of *Oliver Twist*, directed by David Lean.

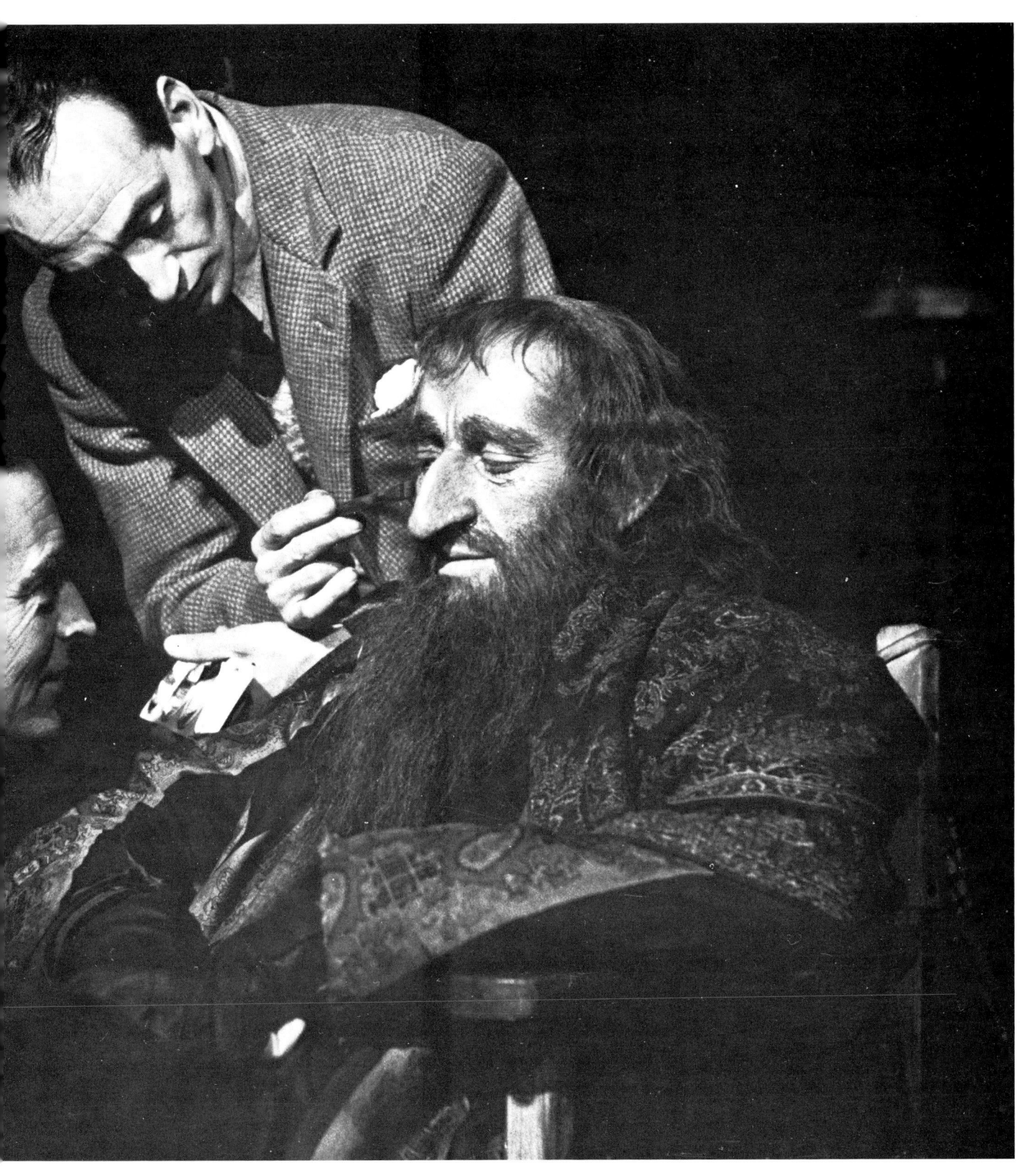

Above The Billy Cotton Band Show, already 22 years old, in full swing at the Coventry Hippodrome in 1953.

Above right The early years of skiffle with Tommy Steel singing in the 'Cats Whiskers' in 1956.

Right A 'one-man band' busker at Hexham in 1950.

NU-SWIFT
1 USE UPRIGH
2 GET NEAR FIR
3 PUSH OVER GUAR
& STRIKE KNO